Fr. Joe ingeniously combines traditional spii
to produce a book which will be very useful
tually and psychologically. It will also help t

Here's a book with a banquet of stories; anecdotes and proverbs to savor again and again like tasty leftovers. Easy to read, spiritual but not pious, profound but practical, Fr. Joe has provided a handbook for anyone eager to experience life in great abundance.

Edward Hays
Author, *Prayers for the Domestic Church*

Fr. Joe relies on years of priestly wisdom to teach us all how to better take care of ourselves. You will feel refreshed and enlightened when you finish this book.

Msgr. Tom Hartman
ABC's *God Squad*

Fr. Joe writes about the ordinary life, about the emotional life, about our struggles and victories, about our heartaches and healings, so engagingly and interestingly, you can't put the book down. A must read for everyone.

Sr. Mary Rose McGready, DC
President, Covenant House

Embracing Change brings us hope, humor, and healing to get through the difficult times.

John Powell, SJ
Author, *Why Am I Afraid to Tell You Who I Am?*

This is an amazing book. It goes right to the heart of what matters most in life with powerful insights. When change is embraced, and you follow Father Joe's ways to a happier and healthier life, each day gets better.

Bobby Rydell
Singer, *Wild One, Sway, Volare*

Fr. Joe's book contains many gold nuggets—a challenging statement here, an amusing incident there, a touching story elsewhere. His suggestions surround these treasures and provide practical self-care tips for living fuller, richer lives.

Joseph M. Champlin
Author, *Together for Life*

I envy Father Joe's students and parishioners. His style, wit, and wisdom apply the eternal truths to contemporary life in a lively way. Don't miss this book.

Mark Link, SJ
Author, *Path Though Scripture*

This user-friendly book will be especially helpful to those seeking a practical plan for personal growth in a spiritual context. Fr. Joe offers a step-by-step plan for living a deeper emotional and spiritual life.

Fran Ferder, FSPA
Author, *Tender Fires: The Spiritual Promise of Sexuality*

This is not the spun sugar servings of so many books but the solid counsel rooted in the deepest biblical experience. Embrace this book and embrace your own life at the same time.

Eugene Kennedy
Author, *9-11: Meditations at the Center of the World*

This book is highly readable, enjoyable, and down to earth. You feel you are visiting with Joe, the way he shares his ideas and stories. His practical suggestions are for everyone who desires to live a fuller and richer life.

Dorothy K. Ederer
Author, *Colors of the Spirit*

Here is a spiritual book that is down to earth, easy to read, full of wisdom, and wonderfully encouraging. I hope you enjoy it as much as I did.

Fr. John Catoir
Author, *God Delights in You*

It's about time the spiritual life was spoken about in a language every believer and non-believer alike can not only understand, but can also find as enjoyable as it is insightful.

Karol Jakowski
Author of *The Silence We Keep: A Nun's View of the Catholic Priest Scandal*

Fr. Joe has woven his quotes and stories into a helpful program for self-care by using humor, challenges, process steps, and his unique "better blockers." It's a fun book to read.

Karen Berry, OSF
Author, "Sowing Seeds" from *Chocolate for a Woman's Courage*

If you feel like you're in a rut and you're in the way, this is the book for you. It presents ten ways to get out of ten common ruts. The key is to embrace the changes—not the ruts.

Andrew Costello, CSSR
Author, *Down to Earth But Looking Up*

Fr. Joe has gathered together his experience and wisdom in a fine book filled with practical and concrete suggestions. His language is plain and everyday; his stories and quotes are worth the book itself.

Edward J. Farrell
Author, *No One Else Can Sing My Song*

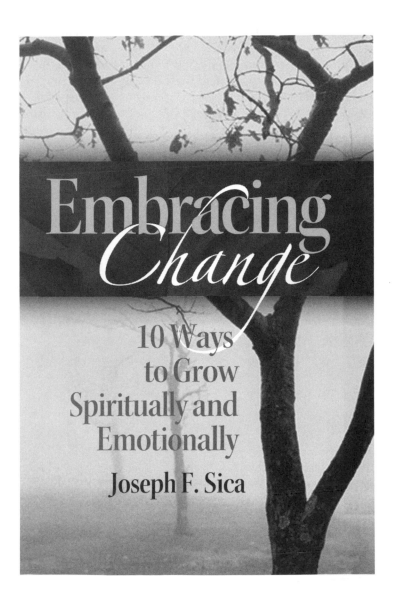

Embracing Change

10 Ways to Grow Spiritually and Emotionally

Joseph F. Sica

TWENTY-THIRD PUBLICATIONS

185 WILLOW STREET • PO BOX 180 • MYSTIC, CT 06355
TEL· 1-800 321-0411 • FAX: 1-800-572-0788
Bayard E-MAIL: ttpubs@aol.com • www.twentythirdpublications.com

Every effort has been made to acknowledge the proper source for the stories used in *Embracing Change*; regrettably, most are unknown. If the source becomes known I will give proper credit in future editions of this book. I would like to give credit, however, to these sources: Page 28-29; "The Rabbi and the Jailer." Harold Kushner; used with permission. Page 62-63; "Hold My Hand, Daddy." Brian Cavanaugh, TOR. *Sower's Seeds of Encouragement,* Mahwah, New Jersey: Paulist Press, 1998. Page 81-82; "The Trouble Tree," (adapted). Brian Cavanaugh, TOR. *Sower's Seeds That Nurture Family Values*. Mahwah, New Jersey: Paulist Press, 2000. Page 96; "Lady, Are You Going To Die?" Leo Buscaglia; used with permission. Page 103; "The Airport Scale," (adapted). Zig Ziglar. *See You At The Top*. Gretna, LA: Pelican Publishers, 1977.

Third printing 2004

Twenty-Third Publications
A Division of Bayard
185 Willow Street
P.O. Box 180
Mystic, CT 06355
(860) 536-2611
(800) 321-0411
www.twentythirdpublications.com

Copyright ©2003 Joseph F. Sica. All rights reserved. No part of this publication may be reproduced in any manner without prior written permission of the publisher. Write to Permissions Editor.

ISBN:1-58595-248-6
Library of Congress Catalog Card Number: 200211197
Printed in Canada

For my sister,
Ann Straneva
I love you.

―――――――

There is no passion to be found playing small—
in settling for a life that is less
than the one you are capable of living.
Nelson Mandela

Contents

Foreword

It was 1978, the beginning of the school year at The Catholic University of America in Washington, D.C., and I was about to begin my third year teaching pastoral care and counseling to Catholic seminarians. The spirit of the Second Vatican Council was very much alive and the University had taken an ecumenical risk and hired me, an ordained Lutheran, to teach in the Theology Department. It was an exciting time in the Church!

My responsibilities were to teach and clinically supervise the ministerial development of seminarians. Into this world of learning to minister to hurting people walked a young seminarian from the Diocese of Scranton, Joe Sica.

My initial impression of this twenty-something seminarian was of a jovial, salt-of-the earth young man who was eager to reach out and connect with people in order to make a difference in their lives and in their relationships with God. Joe was an eager learner. He was able to connect with others by means of his unpretentious attitude and his down to earth approach. He was willing to take appropriate pastoral caring risks in his ministry and people responded to him.

Twenty-four years later, Joe Sica walked back into my life in January 2002. It was the beginning of a new semester at The Catholic University of America, and Joe, on a sabbatical from priestly ministry, was auditing my doctoral course on Marriage and Family Counseling. I was again encountering the same person, although a more mature and developed version of the original, as he entered into the learning process to bring abundance of life in Christ to people in need.

As you read this book, you will encounter the philosophy and practical theology of an educator and parish priest who deeply believes that people can better care for and love themselves in the way that God first loved them. Over and over again you will experience Father Sica's conviction that the Self-Care Solution is "inside work that will bring positive change to the outside of your life." I was gratified to hear Joe make this statement repeatedly in his book. It confirmed for me what I already knew: Joe had listened well when he was a student!

I have been telling ministerial students for years that the power of the first resurrection comes from within the tomb. The power of God, alive in the entombed Christ is the power that rolls away the stone blocking the entrance to the grave. *Embracing Change: 10 Ways to Grow Spiritually and Emotionally*, has the power to help folks who feel burdened, overwhelmed, or spiritually dry to take responsibility and ownership of their lives, and roll away the stone that is blocking a more abundant life from being resurrected. Resurrection begins from the inside out, and this book provides ten ways in which you can risk removing the stones that block your abundant life from being more fully lived.

The master storytelling techniques of Father Sica will enrich you theologically, challenge you spiritually, and connect you deeply with your life.

Let me conclude with a story of my own. Once upon a time there was a person who bought a field that was overgrown with weeds, tall grasses, and bramble bushes. After much hard work that resulted in blisters on the hands and an aching back, the field was cleared, tilled, and planted with beautiful flowers and wonderful vegetables. Showing what had been accomplished to a friend the gardener heard his friend say: "This is a beautiful garden, isn't God wonderful!" The gardener replied, "Yes indeed, God is wonderful, but you should have seen this field when God had it all by himself."

You are about to launch into learning from my friend and former student ten ways you can partner with God so that you can create change, remove clutter, and take greater control of the life that God has given you. I wish you happy and successful gardening.

The Rev. Dr. Charles Gravenstine
Professor of Pastoral Studies,
The Catholic University of America

Preface

In the later years of his life, Pablo Picasso was not allowed to roam an art gallery unattended, for he had been discovered in the act of trying to improve on one of his old masterpieces. Frank Herbert writes: "Without change, something sleeps inside us and seldom awakes. The sleeper must awaken." There's a new life, a new you, waiting to happen all around you. Let it happen.

Embracing Change is a book that is easy to read and apply. Using stories, humor, images, and metaphors, I hope to enhance your experience of living, so you can become fully engaged in life. From sitting down with people over the years and listening to their stories, I've discovered that, although we are all different on the outside, the deeper down we go inside ourselves the more alike we are.

I invite you to journey through these pages with me as your guide. I promise my ten ways to grow spiritually and emotionally will really work if you use them consistently and over time. Trust me. Isaiah (40:31) sums up our destiny: "They that hope in the Lord will renew their strength; they will soar as with eagles' wings. They will run and not grow weary, walk and not grow faint."

God has great plans for you to live a healthy, energetic, and complete life—spiritually and emotionally. Throughout these pages you will find ten ways to live the positive life God offers.

I am blessed to be able to write and publish. It's an honor and privilege that I will never take for granted. As you read through these pages this is my prayer for you along the way:

I yearn to be embraced
in the great hands of your heart—
Oh let them take me now,
into them I place these fragments, my life,
and you, God—spend them however you want.
Rainer Maria Rilke

Acknowledgments

I am amazed as well as humbled by the people who have encouraged and affirmed me along my journey. It is with deep appreciation and gratitude that I thank them here.

Thank you! Joseph and Elveria Sica, my parents, who worked hard all their lives to take care of our needs; never complaining or depriving us of anything. My mother always believed one day I would write a book. One day finally arrived. My parents taught me to be kind to myself and not to do anything to hurt other people. I am thankful for their courage, persistence, and love. They are remarkable.

Their approach to life was simple and logical. My mother would ask: "If he told you to jump off the bridge would you?" I'd answer, "Not again!" And my dad would say, "I can't wait until you grow up and have kids of your own, I hope they do the same to you...." I fooled my dad—I became a priest. They introduced me to God and Jesus. Their positive nurturing faith life enabled me to embrace a God who cares, believes, and will get me through it all. May they enjoy living in God's presence forever.

Thank you! Ann my sister; my entire life. We only have each other now. Our parents have been born into everlasting life and Ann's husband John has joined them, dying at the age of fifty-two. Together we have learned that when things fall apart we need to take the time to heal. Life does come together again, but never as it was before. These family deaths taught me that every moment and all people are precious. Thanks, Ann, for challenging me to approach life with your genuine simplicity, truthfulness, trust, and enthusiasm. I love you so much.

Thank you! Louis and Betty Ann DeNaples, together with your family: Doctors Louis and Lisa, Donna, Margie, Nick, Anne, and Dominica for opening your hearts and home to me and inviting me inside. Each of you, in a unique and personal way, have poured countless riches and meaning into my life which I had no right to expect. Mother Teresa said, "We cannot do great things. We can do small things with great love." Louis, Betty Ann, and their family are living examples of these words. Your love of family, faith, and friends is the measure of your success. Thank you for allowing me the gift of being myself.

Profound gratitude to Gwen Costello, publisher at Twenty-Third for accepting my manuscript for publication. When I received her e-mail in June 2002 saying, "Yes, we will indeed publish your book," the feeling was awesome.

This book would not be possible without the skills of editors and others who assisted me. I appreciate every one of you for helping to polish, refine, and birth *Embracing Change.*

Thank you! Tamar Love, for reading early drafts of the manuscript during my sabbatical at The Catholic University of America. She made my words and thoughts readable. She is very special. Not only is she an exceptional editor and writer, but she has a gentle spirit and heart. With unerring editorial instincts she saw, and helped realize, a vision. Thanks, Tamar, for your constant support of all my writing projects.

Thank you! Mary Carol Kendzia of Twenty-Third Publications, for believing in the message and for always providing quick answers to specific questions. Your energy, enthusiasm, and guidance were wonderful.

Thank you! Debbie McCann, for being a fabulous, efficient, and brilliant editor. Working with you has been a privilege. Thank you for helping me make this book the best it could be.

Thank you! Tracey Selingo, my publicist, who is dedicated, creative, committed, insightful, and indefatigable in her mission.

Thank you! Bishop James C. Timlin whose wisdom and insight, compassion and care, love and leadership have been extended to me throughout my ministry in the Diocese of Scranton.

So often we hear what is wrong with the church. I had the opportunity to hear what is right with the church from teachers like Avery Cardinal Dulles, Monsignor Joseph Kelly, and Reverend Charles Gravenstine. They communicated through word and action an appreciation for our rich Catholic tradition founded by a great Master with a powerful message and a life-giving ministry. Thank you!

Thank you! Father Michael Piccola. You have been a part of my life for over twenty-five years and symbolize for me what ministry is all about: nurturing, energizing, and affirming people through word and sacrament. I admire your integrity and perception, and appreciate your good judgment and advice. Thanks for always being there for me, and for your loyal friendship. I pray God will continue to bless him with many years of ministry as he opens God's word and proclaims good news that fills needs, heals hurts, and brings hope into the everyday stuff and struggles of people's lives.

Thank you! Monsignor Joseph Quinn for your continued encouragement and affirmation. Your notes, cards, and letters always came at a time in my life when I needed them. Thank you for guiding me with great humor, wisdom, and insight.

There are other priest friends I am grateful to: Fathers Joseph Verespy, John Doris, David Betts, Joseph Evanko, Michael Kirwin, John Chmil, and Anthony Tombasco, who have been there for me offering solid advice and warm support when I needed it.

Thank you! Monsignor Donald McAndrews who will be celebrating fifty years of priesthood. I am blessed to be living with him at Saint Aloysius. His enthusiasm and excitement, prayerfulness and gentleness, calmness and peacefulness, in ministry and life, are contagious.

As we grow, people walk into our lives at the right moment, sometimes just to listen, others times to encourage, and still others to challenge. A big thanks to friends, old and new, for their love and patience, especially: Brother James Lemon SJ, Brian Williams, Matthew Solfanelli, William Conaboy, Jr., Byran Boles, Bonnie Wiezavich, Michael Cummings, Gerry Korson, John Burnett, PhD, Joseph Corcoran, Eleanor Brown, Barry Minora, MD, Debbie Waters, Stella Litwin, Susan Barziloski, Ruth Barhight, Edna White, Thomas Kelly, Patricia Kennedy, Stephen, Joanne, Stephen, and Mark Kavulich, Bobby and Camile Ridarelli, Dominica and Angelo Brutico, Salvatore and Susan Cognetti, Michael and Susan Cobb, Robert and Jane Preate, Bruce and Cindy Schoenberg, Bernard and Judy Zipay, Jeff and Beverley O'Lear, Charles and Nancy Kovalchick, Bryan and Katie McGraw, Jack and Patricia DeLeo, Jerry and Liz Morgan, Donald and Jean Sick, Congressman Donald and Carol Sherwood, Anthony and Denise Stella. Thank you for including me in your lives.

To all the young people I've had the privilege of teaching for a dozen years. Beginning at Pocono Central Catholic High School, to Bishop O'Hara High School, and concluding at Bishop Hannan High School, thank you! You have allowed me to step into your lives and see genuine growth in self-awareness, confidence, and faith.

Thank you! To the hundreds of people with whom I have experienced many grace-filled moments in parish ministry at Nativity BVM, Holy Rosary, Saint Peter's Cathedral, Our Lady of the Snows, and now Saint Aloysius. These powerful and life-lifting encounters have strengthened my faith and deepened my experience of God and Jesus who continually welcomes, nourishes, loves, forgives, comforts, and encourages. All of you have been my inspiration; you are why I do what I do.

Well, It's About Time!

The unexamined life is not worth living.
Socrates

Are you living your life the way you want? Or is your life just one regret after another? Have you let the ghosts from the past haunt you? Do you want to kick yourself for not having gone after what you really wanted? How many times have you said, "yes," when deep down you wanted to say, "no"? Are you sorry now you didn't speak out when you had the opportunity to do so? Did you give up after making a mistake because the little voice inside you repeated, over and over, "Forget it, you're a failure. You won't amount to anything."?

Everyone wonders about the hereafter. Think of it this way: what you do here, right now, at this moment, determines what happens after your physical life ends. I believe when you die and stand before God, you will be asked one simple question: "What did you do with the life I gave you?" How will you answer this question? What excuse will you give for refusing to live your life fully? Whom will you blame for your resistance to be you? Imagine how heartbreaking it will be to reach the point of death and realize, "I forgot to live my life."

Well, it's about time for you to take a long look at your life, inside and out, to break down the walls of defensiveness, reluctance, resistance, and fear, so the winds of conversion can blow freely throughout you. Well, it's about time! Hearing these words is an indication you've recognized it's time to change, time to understand yourself better, to see things differently, and decide, "No more, I've had enough. There's got to be another way."

Well, it's about time!

If you've ever heard these words, they've probably come from the mouths of significant, caring people in your life, people who have seen your patterns of living and understood that your habits, compulsions, or addictions were spinning your life out of control, keeping you from letting the real, genuine, authentic you be known and experienced. These caring people hoped you would see where your life was taking you and realize it was time for a change, so they could say in honesty to you: "Well, it's about time!"

Perhaps your friends and loved ones have used different words to convey the same sense of concern:

"Keep it up, and you're headed for danger."

"How much longer are you going to waste your life pleasing people?"

"Can't you see what holding on to the past is doing to you?"

"Chill out—don't take things so seriously!"

"All these years you have taken this abuse, and now look at who you have become."

"You have too much cluttering your life—when are you going to get rid of some of it?"

"This relationship is going nowhere."

"You're letting people take advantage of you."

"You're so naive—you trust too quickly."

"You limit yourself by listening to the critical voices in your life."

Your response may have been defensive: "Stay out of my business. You're just jealous. What do you know, anyway?"

You may have been acting out a script written and directed by someone else, or allowed a bad habit to run your life, rendering it out of control and unmanageable. Your loved ones' words may have come across as arrogant, with an "I told you so" attitude, but if you listen, you'll hear they're really saying: "Hey, open your eyes! You can do better. You can change things, and create the life you want to live. It's possible."

The Self-Care Solution
You're probably saying to yourself, "Just what I need—another self-help book." Bookstore shelves are filled with manuals that tell you how to live your life, everything from how to be more organized to how to

be a happier person, from how to improve your relationship to how to be a better parent. If you aren't careful, it's very easy to feel intimidated by all this advice!

While self-help books offer ways to live the good life, not every book is for every person. If you try to read them all, you'll be too inundated with information to manage any real change. Instead of another self-help fix, this book offers a Self-Care Solution, a program that isn't about changing who you fundamentally are, but revealing the person you want—and were meant—to be.

The Self-Care Solution is a ten-step process, outlined in each chapter of this book:

Embracing change: Self-care is allowing change into your life and giving yourself permission to tend to yourself, making your happiness and quality of life a top priority.

Clearing out clutter: Self-care is putting your insides in order and watching the difference it will make on the outside.

Taking control of your life: Self-care is taking a back seat to no one and really believing that you are the driving force in your life.

Finding a cure for the disease to please: Self-care is taking the pressure off yourself to live the way others want you to live, sharing what is going inside and not acting opposite to what you are feeling, just to be loved.

Letting go and learning to forgive: Self-care is letting go of the past and learning to live your life for today and tomorrow. Self-Care is learning to forgive yourself and others and not allowing past mistakes to rule your life.

Connecting with others: Self-care is connecting to each other in healthy relationships and talking to each other with words that bring out the best in one another, allowing each other to express what is going on inside.

Casting away heartache: Self-care is knowing what to do when life hands you trouble, pain, and heartache, and understanding that it's okay to laugh and enjoy all the pleasures life has to offer.

Overcoming adversity: Self-care is learning from adversity, not falling beneath it; it's finding the positive, not dwelling on the negative.

Talking with the shepherd: Self-care is surrendering yourself to God through prayer and letting God help you through the difficult parts of your life.

Believing the best is yet to come: Self-care is accepting the death of a loved one and finding the courage to face the rest of your life, believing this life is just the first step to the hereafter, which is better than anything you can imagine.

The Self-Care Solution is a spiritual renovation of yourself, a way of moving toward "wholly"-ness: togetherness and fullness in your life, with all aspects of yourself and your life integrated together into a whole. Like all renovations, you will not be destroying what is already there, just improving, updating, and changing yourself, making yourself stronger and more attractive so you can experience harmony, balance, and completeness in your life.

The Self-Care Solution is "inside work" that will bring positive changes to the outside of your life. Watch the difference. When you develop a good sense of yourself and come to know and love the person God has made you to be, it will affect what happens to the rest of your life. You will find that you respond, instead of reacting, to the positive and negative forces in your life. Things around you may collapse, but you will have the inner resources to hold yourself together and act responsibly.

The Self-Care Solution will put you in touch with the God inside you, a God who wants you to always remember that you're God's child, a God of unconditional love, who calls you each day to take God inside your life and let God know what is going on so God can help.

Better Blockers

At the end of each chapter, I will give you some "Better Blockers." Let me explain with a story: A young man was visiting New York City for the first time. Astonished by the skyscrapers and the crowds, he needed directions to the city landmarks, so he stopped an elderly woman, asking, "How do you get to Carnegie Hall?" The woman paused and replied, "Practice, young man, practice." Better blockers are your daily practice, reminders to encourage you to keep practicing the Self-Care Solution each day and never quit improving yourself and the quality of life you deserve.

When you find yourself slipping into old routines you've worked hard to improve with the Self-Care Solution, don't get discouraged. Turn to the end of each chapter and read the Better Blocker, an extra thought for you to take along with you to remind you not to block your life with disappointments, demands, worries, resentments, grudges, negative attitudes, superior feelings, and regrets, but to believe God wants nothing but the good life for you.

The Self-Care Solution for Living the Good Life
If you read this book with an open mind and the willingness to improve yourself, then you will find my book helpful. Throughout, I will focus on the question, "Are you embracing the gift of you and giving yourself permission to fully engage in living life?" We'll take a look at different ways you can learn to live your life more fully, inviting God into your heart and learning how to be yourself, always.

As I walk you through your life, I will offer stories, lessons, questions, and experiences to guide you along your journey, helping you embrace yourself and reclaim the quality of life and love you so richly deserve. I hope each chapter will recharge your batteries and keep you going when you feel lousy, drained, and overwhelmed by life. I hope this book will be a soul booster to get you through life's difficulties, which can often seem to get the better of you.

As you work through the Self-Care Solution, remember to applaud yourself for the progress you've made. If you apply yourself, changes and growth will happen in your life; you'll be proud, feel better, get along with others more easily, and believe God's love will turn crosses into resurrections.

Well, it's about time to shake yourself up, wake yourself up, and introduce you to the stranger living inside—you—and live the way you want to, with integrity, responsibility, and happiness. Life is a gift waiting to be unwrapped and lived abundantly with every breathe you take, so what are you waiting for?

Embracing Change

Remember that it may be all right to be content with what you have,
but never with what you are. There's always room for improvement
—it's the biggest room in the house.
Louise Heath Leber

The Self-Care Solution begins with a reflection on this wonderful passage from Saint Paul's Letter to the Hebrews (12:1): "Let us strip off and lay aside everything that holds us back."

Everybody dies, but not everybody lives. Start by looking at what keeps you from living freely. So much clutter has gotten in the way, holding you back from being fully alive. So much of you still needs to be revealed and lived. When you understand what it is, it's decision time—either stay the way you have been or make adjustments so you can come to know and love the preciousness of who you are, a skillful masterpiece of God.

Jesus spent forty days in the desert facing demons. It's time to go into the desert inside yourself and encounter your own demons. And who are they? Here are just a few:

The Underminer Demon. Using words that leave you feeling depressed and defeated, the Underminer Demon is out to sabotage you and discount your self-worth. Sarcasm, cutting, slicing, dicing, back-stabbing, gossiping, embellishing, labeling, name-calling, singling-out, and comparing fill the Underminer Demon's arsenal, weapons to reduce you and make you feel bad about yourself.

Underminer Demons are all around you; they may appear to have an interest in you, but deep down they want to undermine you as a means of controlling you and making themselves feel more powerful. Listen to the way they speak to you: what kind of words do they use? Do they build you up as a person, or bring you down? Are they a drain, taking all the energy out of you, deflating and wiping you out; a pain, saying words that wound and hurt you deeply; or a strain, making it hard to like yourself? You've been taught to respond with, "Sticks and stones may break my bones, but words can never harm me." Wrong. The Underminer Demons have only one purpose when they talk to you or about you: to devastate you as a dignity-filled human person.

The Reminder Demon. Partners with the Underminer Demon, Reminder Demons create shame and guilt in your life by pushing buttons connected to the past. They reinforce everything the Underminer Demons have told you, hitting you over the head and reminding you about your scars, sins, wrongs, mistakes, blunders, missed opportunities, bad decisions, and improper choices.

The longer you pay attention to them the more havoc they'll bring into your life. They'll keep coming at you with: "remember when?" or "don't forget the time you...."

The Distractor Demon. Distractor Demons want to keep you off course. They want you to follow someone else and will subtly distract you by filling your head with the way you should live your life: through pleasing others, excessively worrying over hurts, troubles, and heartaches, or being serious all the time.

The first step toward embracing change is for you to look inside yourself and name the demons that have stolen your joy for living life, obscuring the way you desire to live. Well, it's about time you begin to face these demons and tell them to be quiet. It's time to exorcise them out of your life, to clear out, get rid of, dump, do away with, and abandon everything that has prevented you from knowing yourself, everyone who has worn the guise of one of these demons.

A warrior was standing face to face with an old monk. With sword raised he said, "I could run this sword through you and you would die." The monk said without blinking, "I know you can. But only if I let you."

Keep this in mind when the three demons appear in your life attempting to undermine, remind, or distract you. They only have the power to succeed if you let them.

They want to fill your head with nonsense. The more you listen the worse you will feel. Change the inner dialogue with yourself. Self-talk does affect how you feel. Override their nasty and negative comments with words of encouragement that ring true for you. For example, when you mess up, the reminder demon will say, "What did you expect, you can't do anything right!" Replace it with "I'm strong and capable" or "I can succeed; I've done it before and I'll do it again." You need to decide, "enough already," and walk away. Stop giving these demons an audience. Kick these demons out of your life.

As you face your demons, you will begin to take ownership of your life and responsibility for yourself. You will discover the gift you are and the gifts you have, and create a rich, meaningful life.

Know Yourself, Inside and Out

Saint Teresa of Avila used to say, "Almost all the problems in the spiritual life stem from a lack of self-knowledge." Self-knowledge is the foundation for the renovation of you. When you are in touch with what is going on inside, you are able to make better decisions. If you ignore what is going on inside, you can make unintentional choices and decisions. Then the string of regrets begins— "Why did I do that?"

When you know yourself, you begin to recognize long-standing negative patterns: letting others direct your life, staying stuck in the past, pleasing others, being unable to handle the unfairness of life, forgetting to relax, putting off saying "I love you," not enjoying the gift of life, just making it through the day and not feeling alive, keeping bitterness, anger, and resentment blooming, plus so much more. All these negative thoughts and feelings are food for the three demons, keeping them well fed and encouraging them to stick around.

Knowing yourself isn't easy. It's going to be a time of self-disclosure for you as you explore your inner world and share it with others. It's risky to allow others inside your personal world, so you may have been putting off these renovations for a while, playing it safe because you were afraid others would find out what you are made of. Or you may simply not share your feelings, hopes, dreams, disappointments, and fears because you haven't yet learned how to express them. You are never too old to begin and learn. Right now is your chance to start. If not today, then when? Tomorrow? Tomorrow may never come.

The artist Paul Cézanne tells us, "Right now, a moment of time is passing by...we must become that moment." You have today, this moment, to get started and see what can happen. Meet your fears and work to renovate yourself.

What's your greatest fear? That you will share your vulnerable spots and someone may use them to hurt you? Perhaps you're afraid that when you look inside yourself, you will discover someone you can't live with for the rest of your life. It may feel like you are living with a stranger, someone you aren't sure you want to know.

It's okay to be afraid, but don't let your fear control you. If you choose not to explore what's going on inside, you will never experience the richness of opening up your life, looking inside, working on what keeps you from feeling good about yourself, and having your goodness affirmed by another person who cares.

"Know thyself" is a well-known axiom of the ancients, who were very smart! Well, it's about time to be yourself, first by finding out who you are, and then by cultivating the willpower to be this self. Get deep inside yourself and find and cherish the treasure of you—an irreplaceable creation of God.

The Self-Care Solution is about tending to your soul. The outside is only a vehicle that carries around what is essential: who you are on the inside, you as you, no games to play to keep others at a distance, no masks to pretend you are somebody else, the indisputable you—a renovated, changed, and renewed you.

The real, genuine, authentic you has always been there, waiting to come out of the dark. Clutter, giving the power of your life over to somebody else, the compulsion to feel inferior, heartaches, hurts, always pleasing, wasting time on the small stuff, keeping grudges alive, staying attached to the past, forgetting life is about living, limiting your attitude through distorted thinking, letting others walk all over you—all these demons have kept you from knowing this real you on your journey to wholly-ness.

It's been too long since you paid attention to what is going on inside you and your life. You owe it to yourself to change things. Begin to take responsibility for the life you have been given by God. It's the only one you've got! If you don't start looking out for yourself, who will? You have a right to pamper yourself with inside care, gentleness, and understanding. So go ahead and do it!

Life isn't a dress rehearsal. It's the real thing. You have never seen today before, so don't let it slip away into history without making some difference in yourself. Jackie Robinson says, "Life is not a spectator sport. If you're going to spend your whole life in the grandstand, just watching what goes on, in my opinion you're wasting your life." I agree. Life moves forward, with or without you. It's not going to wait and say, "Whenever you're ready." It's inviting you—now—to come on board.

You may have allowed yourself to be covered with layers of self-doubt from years of neglect and lack of attention. It's time to get to work and journey inside with these tools:

- confidence: "I can do this";
- desire: "I want to do this"; and
- determination: "I will do this."

Then watch the miracle of you resurrect.

Mirror the Inner You

As I said previously, as you grow and change, your exterior world becomes a reflection of your interior. The renovation of the you inside will change how you respond to what happens outside you. It's not complicated. Dr. Karl Menninger once said about relationships: "Getting close to others begins with one's own inner self." You must first come to know yourself and what's going on inside of you before you enter an intimate relationship with another person. When you know yourself, you can relate to others more effectively.

Change takes time. After years of avoidance, be patient but not lazy. Get on your feet and take some action. Sure, it's not going to happen overnight. Once you start you will see that change comes slowly, but stay with it by chanting, "I will, I will," and then believe it will happen. Keep this quote in your mind: "Inch by inch, it's a cinch." Once you see a different you coming out, you will get hooked on changing more and more, eventually reaching a point in your life when you feel comfortable inside your skin, standing up proudly and saying, "I like who I am." This affirmation, which can only come from inside you, will bring peace into your life, strong conviction about your decisions, and a positive connection with those you love.

When you finish the journey, you will have a healthier picture of who you are, colored by freedom to express what you think and feel, together with an endorsement of your own individuality, better skills for getting along with others, and possession of the belief that God does care about creation—everything and everyone in the world, and the struggles that they will encounter on the journey. So, don't you agree that it's about time to reveal the inner you?

Just because you've always done something a certain way, it doesn't mean it's the right way to do things. You might test this idea by trying to remember why you started doing something a certain way and thinking about whether or not those same reasons still hold true. Take the following story.

> Once upon a time a little girl watched her mother prepare the ham for Easter dinner. The mother took the ham and cut off both ends before putting it into the pan. Her daughter asked, "Mommy, why did you do that?"
>
> The mother replied, "That's the way my mother did it and it always tasted delicious, so I don't want to change the recipe."
>
> The little girl was persistent in her need to find out the reason for this ritual, so she asked her grandmother. "Grandma, when you cooked the ham for Easter why did you cut off both ends before putting it into the pan?"
>
> "Well, sweetheart, if I remember, that Easter the ham was too big for the pan."

To be truthful, you have to admit you would like to change some things about your life, especially those habits and behaviors you are not happy with—yelling, being incapable of controlling your temper, bursting out in anger—all because you don't feel you are in charge of your life. Perhaps you take everything too seriously. Does this sound like you?

"It's been so long that I can't remember the last time I had a good laugh. It's so hard to relax."

"I need to get around to making that visit and saying those words, 'I love you.'"

You might always be looking at life out of the rear-view mirror, wondering where it went and what just happened. Maybe you want to change your tendency toward impatience, or the fact you cannot admit you were wrong, or your tendency to hold grudges. Maybe it is a relationship that needs some work: the intimacy isn't there, feelings have been violated, you feel you just don't matter, communication has broken down, and both of you are growing in different directions.

The Self-Care Solution is about change, being open to new possibilities for making your life worthwhile and meaningful. You must learn how to handle change; it is one of the basics of human life that people want most, fear most, and need most. Change is never easy. Change is frightening. Change takes time. Change means making mistakes. A change means first unlearning, then relearning how to do something differently. Change is risky. It's admitting there is another way—sometimes a better way.

Face your fear of change by beginning to look deep inside yourself. Come out of the dark corners of yourself and step into the light. Risk this new experience. I know it is safe to stay as you are, hiding in your comfort zone. Welcome this new challenge. Deep down, you know you deserve more. Well, it's about time to believe you have the ability to get it.

Change is healthy. You need it to grow. It is unhealthy to cling to old habits and old ways of relating that just don't work any longer. Change brings newness and freshness into your life and relationships, enabling you to solve problems and grow in new directions.

Spring Cleaning

Spring gives cues for change. It's clean-up time, time to repair or replace what the winter weather has damaged. It's longer days. It's planting time. The springtime is a chance for some to say, "The winter exercising program paid off, so let me see what fits and doesn't fit."

The same holds true for the renovation of you. Look deep within and clean up the jumble that has prevented you from being yourself. Notice what hasn't contributed to your growth as a human person and do away with it. The habits or behaviors, the attitudes or addictions, the past or the people—all need to be repaired or replaced. Pull them out of the nooks and crannies inside yourself and look at how you have allowed them to rule your life.

For Christians, Spring also brings the celebration of Easter, a wonderful metaphor for your journey to renovation. Before the sun rises, there is darkness; before the resurrection, there is the cross; before Sunday morning, there is Good Friday. The journey at first will seem difficult. It is. You are used to the way you have been living and relating. Change will seem impossible at first.

Now is your chance to go inside the tomb of you, where it is cold, dark, and spooky. You will encounter the demons that have undermined you, distracted you, and deceived you from discovering the splendidness of you. Enter the tomb and work through all that has held you back for years, allowing Jesus to call you out as he did Lazarus. Once in the light, Jesus will untie you from all that has bound you.

As you come to a clearer vision and understanding of yourself, you will begin to notice there are people who just don't want to change. They stop growing. They stay stuck in their tombs, and when the voice of Jesus calls them to come out of the dark into the light, they huddle down in the corner, hoping Jesus will go away. They become blind and deaf to how their life has lost its luster. Their behavior hurts people, alienating others and driving them away. Family and friends avoid them as they stay the way they are, never changing, never growing. What a misfortune. It doesn't have to be this way. You have the power to change. All need you to do is to choose wisely.

Will-Power or Won't-Power?

Won't-power. The force behind it is to complain and blame your inability to change on others and any circumstances that fit your behavior:

> "I'm not gonna change. This is the way I've always been."
> "Tough. I'm not gonna do anything differently."
> "I won't even consider it."
> "I always had these habits and I am gonna have them until I die."
> "I have always done it this way, why change?"

"My mother/father made me do it," or "My husband/wife insists on it this way."

"I didn't have a good education and never got any breaks."

There is also another power: will-power.

"I want to get better."

"I want to improve."

"I want to listen more and fight less."

"I want to take control of who I am and where I want to grow."

"I want to laugh again."

"I want to stop living in my history and start living now."

"I want to have someone I can run to when it all comes tumbling down."

"I want to be in a happy, working relationship that mutually fulfills our needs."

"What do I have to do for things to get better?"

"Will you support and encourage me during my change?"

"I was blind. I didn't realize how I was living life and the direction it took."

The force behind will-power is a deep-down desire to take charge, to take responsibility for your life and admit change can renovate you. It makes you a better person and your relationships stronger.

Katharine Hepburn sums it up well when she says: "If you want to change, you're the one who has got to change. Take responsibility for every area of your life. It's as simple as that, isn't it?"

Will-power gives you the ability to change and experience the newness and freshness of living life with the attitude of, "Well, it's about time, so let's get to work!"

Better Blocker

Jason ordered a floral arrangement for the grand opening of his friend's deli. When Jason arrived at the deli, he was shocked to see his arrangement bore the ribbon: "Rest in Peace." Furious, he returned to his office, called the florist, and complained. The florist said, "Relax. Somewhere in the city today there is a person being buried under a floral arrangement that reads: 'Good Luck In Your New Location.'"

The Self-Care Solution is about location, location, location. Before you can experience change, you must locate yourself in the present, within yourself. The Self-Care Solution is the journey that begins when you believe: I want to change because there is more in life waiting for me.

Clearing Out Clutter

The simplified life is a Holy Life. Much more calm, much less stress.
Peace Pilgrim

Jesus is coming to your house for dinner. The family is excited. Everything is ready. He arrives and before everyone eats, he wants to see your home. You take Jesus from room to room. He loves it and you're happy. Jesus asks, "Can I peek in your closets?"

Thinking to yourself, "Closets? Clutter!" You respond, "Jesus, how about another time?" Jesus replies, "No, let me look inside now. Then I'll look in all the drawers."

No matter how clean your house seems, if there's clutter hidden away, then you're going to seem a poor housekeeper. But when you clean out the clutter, making changes on the inside of your life, your whole self will feel cleaner, stronger, and better. You will have become a good housekeeper of your own life, clearing out the dust bunnies instead of sweeping them under the carpet.

Clutter affects every part of your life: your ability to think clearly, feel deeply, spend quality time with family, stay focused in prayer, and get along with people. Clutter makes you frustrated, edgy, upset, angry, and unhappy. When you do something about it, your life will change, becoming peaceful, relaxed, and happy.

Begin by looking inside yourself at what you need to give up—addictions, unpleasant behaviors, bad habits, or unfinished business. Facing your clutter and tossing it out of your life frees you and releases you. It doesn't smother you any longer. You have room to grow.

If you've been carrying around unresolved feelings, they will seep into your daily living and your attitudes concerning life, affecting how you relate with people. Unresolved feelings just don't disappear—what goes unresolved will not dissolve—they just come out in other forms of behavior that can ruin relationships and make life miserable.

Unfinished business is the excess baggage you have been keeping in storage all your life. You don't need it. It's there because you haven't done anything about it. It's dusty and it takes up space because you have chosen to ignore it. You may have tripped over it many times. You live with the hope it will disappear. Too bad—it won't.

Excess baggage exhausts you and tires you out. It drains your energy and dampens your enthusiasm. It creates distance in your relationships. It's in the way, preventing the real, genuine authentic you from coming out. Put away unfinished business for good, so you can have the room to grow. When you do, you will feel lighter, freer, and happier.

These steps will help you face what you have been avoiding—getting rid of clutter pile-up. Follow four easy steps:

Originate. How did the clutter get into your life? Trace its origins: thoughts, comments, memories, or actions you can't shake loose. Be honest with yourself, and look until you find the true source of your clutter.

Articulate. Go inside the desert of yourself and name your clutter. This may be difficult to do, so here are some suggestions to get you started:

• Is your clutter gossiping, complaining, judging, envy, lying, stealing or cursing?

• Do you worry with "what-if" thinking, exaggerating things out of proportion, crossing bridges before you get to them, and carrying your problems as you would companions?

• Do you live your life the way others think you should live it?

• Are you too serious about everything, unable to lighten up?

• Do you expect and fear the worst, reliving yesterday?

• Do you book yourself on guilt trips, beating yourself up over mistakes and demanding perfection?

• Are you being unfaithful to your marriage vows?

• Do you have problems with drinking, smoking, gambling, or drug addiction?

• Are you taking on too much, so that your relationships and prayer life suffer?

Articulating your laundry list of clutter helps you identify the problems you wish to be rid of. Again, be honest with yourself!

Investigate. How is the clutter affecting your life and relationships? Do you find it hard to concentrate? Are you nervous, anxious, and uptight? Has the clutter turned you into a person others don't want to be around because they feel you're preoccupied, distracted, and distant?

Eliminate. It's decision time. You know the clutter by name; you see where it came from and what it's doing to your life. The next step is to give it up and find the willpower to keep it out of your life. Once you eliminate the clutter, your mind will be cleared, your life improved, and you'll get along better with other people.

Examine your life, and then write down a list of the stuff you want to eliminate, your clutter list. Next to each item, write how you will give it up. For example, you have a tendency to always believe the worst is going to happen—when the telephone rings, you're expecting it's going to be bad news. How will you eliminate this piece of clutter? Brainstorm a few different ways and pick the one you think will work the best.

Look at your clutter and don't procrastinate. It takes determination and truthfulness to face your clutter and say, "Well it's about time I do something about it." Be patient—it doesn't happen overnight! Bring Jesus into your mess; turn it over to him, and pray, "Lord, wipe out the clutter that confuses my life so I can change and live better." Pray, "Jesus, separate what I am from what I am not, because I have allowed clutter to rule my life."

I love the scene in Luke's gospel (10:38–47), when Jesus visits Martha and Mary. Martha's clutter is expressed in her attitude: "Lord, don't you care that my sister has left me by myself to do the serving?" Anger and frustration from too many demands distress Martha. Jesus's response is great: "Martha, you're anxious and worried about many things." In other words, "Martha, calm down and loosen up."

Decide, "Yes, I am going to spiritually clean out the closets and drawers of my life by eliminating the clutter." If you stay dedicated to removing it, you will see changes that last.

As you keep looking inside to see what clutter you need to give up, read the Sermon on the Mount (Matthew: 5 to 7). It's all about the clutter that gets in your way.

The Sermon takes into consideration all the attitudes that can clutter your life and make it difficult for you to find happiness. Vengeance, worry, judging others, explosive anger, holding grudges, possessions, inability to make up your mind, crossing boundaries in relationships, obsession with wealth and power, bragging, cynicism, feelings of superiority, lack of trust, always being right, "my way is the only way," talking down to people, and lying—it's all clutter that you will eventually see you need to be rid of. De-clutter your life by practicing the directives Jesus gives in his sermon:

- Reach out for help
- Build bridges in relationships
- Organize your priorities
- Tell the truth
- Give people another chance
- Bounce back from pain
- Work from love
- Believe in the remarkableness of you
- Know you have God on your side

Trying to live your life when it is filled with clutter is like building your house on sand: when the rains fall, floods arrive, and winds blow, it will collapse and be completely ruined. When I allow myself to have these attitudes in my life, I know I am headed for isolation. People will distance themselves from me. Without the conviction to change, I end up alone and lonely. The Sermon on the Mount names the clutter and equips you with convictions and courage not to let it take over your life and destroy you.

Talk, Think, and Take
When you exaggerate your worst fears and messiest bits of clutter, they

come out of hiding and start to get the best of you, bringing with them a chorus of negative voices you'll hear in your head.

Some ways to combat this chorus:

- Talk back to yourself and tell the committee of voices to shut up. Be positive in your talk.
- Think possibilities and not problems. When you notice yourself being overwhelmed by thoughts that seem to be negative and pessimistic, stop the thoughts and replace them with positive possibilities.
- Take ownership of your life and don't let forces or fears saddle your life with unnecessary clutter. When you achieve the results you want in your life, bring out another piece of clutter and get rid of it. Repeat as necessary.

You'll know when your clutter list is shrinking by the change in your behavior, in the way you relate to people, and how you now respond to different situations. In the past, the clutter didn't contribute to your life; it controlled it. Since you've focused, concentrated, and persisted in your commitment for positive changes, you've managed your clutter.

When a problem arises, instead of rummaging through your clutter to find the resource you need to manage the situation, you'll be able to respond calmly and ask yourself, "What am I going to do about this?" You can talk to others without losing your composure. You understand the damage caused by impulsive reactions of lying, striking back, or acting from anger, and now you've gotten a taste of how good it feels to be clutter-free from these negative forces. You promise yourself to work each day to de-clutter and keep yourself on the path of good living.

God can help you eliminate and manage your clutter. As you progress, try one of the following:

- Visit your church and sit in Jesus's presence for a holy hour, during which time you cannot be disturbed. Bring your clutter list with you and turn it over to Jesus for help.
- Read the lives of the saints, a book about brothers and sisters who struggled with clutter, and learn that you're not alone.

• Pray: "Jesus, it is not the clutter in plain sight that nags me, but the hidden clutter. It's those sins that I cannot keep up with—those petty little grievances, the grudges, the superior attitudes, thoughts, and feelings that no one else knows about but you. Help me to clean my heart, removing all pride, ill feelings, and prejudice. The clutter in my real closets will never hurt anyone. The clutter in my heart will. Amen."

Don't be so naive to think clutter can't slip back into your life when you aren't looking. That's why it's so important to periodically make a clutter list and review your life in order. Clutter will always be there, but you don't have to let it dominate your life.

Better Blocker

See yourself as a collection of "clutter in recovery." People often think of recovery in terms of addictions to alcohol, drugs, or gambling. Clutter can also be addictive. When it goes unnoticed and unattended, it can make your life unmanageable. People can be hurt and relationships fractured. Once you admit you are powerless over your clutter and take positive steps to bring it under control, your life will change for the better.

Three words will help you: focus, concentration, and persistence. Focus on how clutter is directing your behavior; concentrate on ways to tame it and reduce it; and be persistent—never give up but stick with it.

Always remember that "expression" is the opposite of "depression." When you express what your clutter is doing to you, you no longer feel ruled by it. You're on your way to eliminating it from your life. Talk with someone, write down your clutter list, and release all the excess baggage that fills your life.

Taking Control of Your Life

In life we are to lift up others; not push them down.
Brian Cavanaugh

Once upon a time, there lived a beautiful young girl named Rapunzel, who lived in a tower with a nasty witch. Every day Rapunzel was told by the witch, "Rapunzel, you are ugly, ugly, ugly." Rapunzel was in fact beautiful, but she failed to notice her prettiness because the witch repeatedly told her how ugly she was.

The repeated messages of the witch made her a P.O.W.—a Prisoner of Words. The witch stood in Rapunzel's way of freedom and of seeing her own attractiveness. Because of the witch's continued put-downs, Rapunzel was a prisoner of her own imagined ugliness, unable to break free of the negative thoughts that bound her.

Rapunzel isn't able to be herself or like herself, to take charge of her own life. She listens to the judgmental voices that intimidate, creating feelings of inferiority, self-doubt, and inadequacy. Rapunzel's story is about staying stuck in old ways of relating that just don't work any longer, nursing old hurts, refusing to forgive and begin again, and avoiding growth at any costs. It's becoming too comfortable with the way you are, even though you know there is another way. It's staying in the dark out of laziness, weakness, and fear, refusing to take control of yourself.

The light side of the story is what happens when Rapunzel finally sees herself as she truly is: she likes who she is and realizes she is in charge of her life, finding that she can live it the way she wants. She kicks out of her life all those people who stand in the way of growth, learning to be free of the past that is useless and unreal, forgiving herself and healing wounds that prevent her from living fully. The light side of Rapunzel's story represents the renovations we need to do inside...the third step of the Self-Care Solution.

Rapunzel's story offers us a renovation choice: remain chained and stay "just as you are," or change and become "who you really are." You can be Rapunzel, easily trading places with her and putting yourself in the story. You are Rapunzel every time you have failed to see your God-given magnificence, significance, value, and richness as a uniquely created human person. You are Rapunzel when you have lived in the dark and allowed all those nasty witches to layer you in self-doubt and sabotage your self-worth. You think and feel, "I am not good enough, pretty enough, or smart enough." You are Rapunzel when you are a P.O.W., listening to all those messages that didn't build you up, but were critical and cutting, holding you back from growing into the masterpiece God made you to be.

Look at your life. Who are the witches? You know them by name: people who remind you of a past hurt or a failure; critical people who are always finding fault and taking you back to the way you were. They attack, judge, and blame you when things go wrong. They like beating you up for the smallest mistake. They like reducing you to the simplest terms and most convenient definitions of who you are. Often the criticizers feel better about themselves by putting you down.

You know the type—the person who can spot a flaw from across the room, gives unsolicited advice, frequently complains and passes, and seems impossible to please.

Unfortunately, by the time the critics are finished with you, your self-esteem is shot to pieces and you feel totally unlovable, unacceptable, and incapable of anything positive. Look at what they've done and the price you've paid: they've used your past as a weapon to put you down. They may even call you names: dumb, stupid, ugly, weak, incompetent. They are busy undermining your self-esteem and taking away any good feelings you have about yourself. Layer upon layer of feelings of inadequacy and inferiority cover you and your real, genuine, authentic self is lost.

Stinkin' Thinkin'

When people who are important to you repeat these negative messages over and over, they're hard to shake loose from your mind. You begin to believe things that aren't true about yourself. I call it "stinkin' thinkin'." It's dangerous. As you think it, you feel it, and as you feel it, you act it out.

You didn't arrive in the world with these thoughts. You didn't develop a put-down vocabulary on your own. Somewhere on your journey of life, a significant person—a teacher, coach, parent, brother, sister, spouse, or friend—put these negative thoughts in your head.

The attack may have been a direct hit: "You're dumb!" Or a comparison, "Your sister always made us proud." How you feel about yourself is equal to the amount of criticisms or build-ups you received throughout your life. Until you can face the witches in your life who stand in your way, you will always feel less than you are and never realize the potential of who you can become.

No physical chains bind you. The chains are made in your mind and locked with your own thoughts. You have allowed people to contribute each link of the chain. A comment, a statement, or a remark you just can't get out of your head all create a change that cripples you and keeps you from taking steps out of the dark and into the light.

If your thoughts can bind you, they can also free you. The critics create cornerstones of guilt and feelings of inadequacy, which so many have built their lives and relationships around. You need to disarm them. Stop listening to them. Override all the negative talk that has choked you with positive thoughts about yourself. When you talk back to yourself, you erase what has been put there and what you have allowed to remain. You have the willpower to unlock the chain and break it.

Rapunzel had her Well-It's-About-Time moment when a prince, the cultivator, called Rapunzel to come out of the tower, encouraging her to throw out her hair so he could climb up. Rapunzel's eyes opened, giving her a reflection of herself in the prince's eyes and allowing her to discover her true beauty.

Look at your life. Who are the princes? You know them by name: all those people during your life who have come out of the crowd and stepped forward to remind you, well, it's about time. The princes are those significant, caring people who see you as a present-moment miracle, always in the process of growing, learning, and changing. They are nurturing and cultivating people who offer constructive ways to improve your life, supporting you through kindness, gentleness, patience, understanding, and acceptance. They push aside the past and focus on the present, which is loaded with so many possibilities.

Look at what they've done for you: they've encouraged you to let go of a bad habit or unpleasant behavior, as you come to the decision, "I don't want to live this way any longer; I want to change." Using willpower, you can.

The core qualities that are essential to cultivators are: patience, commitment, optimism, tolerance, and perseverance. They are available, inspiring, and unconditionally supportive. And because of the loving boost from the cultivators you had the potential to develop inner strength and grow as a healthy, caring person.

Hang out with cultivators who have a positive impact in your life. And while you're at it, dump those critical friends of yours. Nurturing people walk in and make the room light up and they'll make you feel unique, special, and good about yourself. Criticizers are derogatory and judgmental—they're like the energy vampires of the universe.

Be Yourself

Too often you are busy making yourself over to fit in and be accepted. You crave the approval of others and often ignore your own worth. You put yourself on hold. Accept you. Love you. Grow each moment into the person God created you to be: one-of-a-kind, unique, unrepeatable, special, and precious in God's sight.

Judy Garland summed it up best: "Be a first-rate edition of yourself, rather than a second-rate edition of somebody else." Well, it's about time to believe and be convinced that "you" are the only "you" in the whole history of personkind. You have already wasted too much time trying to measure up to other people's expectations, losing your own self in the process.

Be you. Cherish your God-given worth and dignity. You have intrinsic value because you are God's child. When you learn to love yourself and be yourself, it frees you from all distractions and lets the present moment unfold to you all the wonders it holds.

Be you. Look inside and discover the richness and splendor that makes you a limited edition, a masterpiece. To settle for anything less is wrong.

Anita, a friend of mine, had everything going for her. Extremely attractive, insightful, intelligent, and talented, Anita disarmed everyone she met. She had no agenda about people. She would sit and listen to their stories. She was pleasant, kind, and gentle, yet I always sensed she had a restless spirit. If she had one flaw, it was that she never believed in herself, even though she had won a battle with cancer during her high school years and went on to finish college.

After college, Anita's life was a roller coaster ride. She was Rapunzel, trapped in a tower of, "What am I going to do with my life? Who will love me and what do I have to do to get them to appreciate me? Who do I need to please to be loved and feel like I matter?" She couldn't find her place in the world. She would continually make herself over and try any new fad for approval. One day, life became too much for Anita. On a Monday afternoon, she put a gun to her head and decided to end her life. She survived a few days in the hospital with severe brain damage, and then died at the end of the week.

Anita had princes in her life who deeply loved her, who reminded her of her inner magnificence, but she didn't believe them and she didn't listen to their voices. Instead, she listened to others who stripped away any good feelings she could have had about herself.

You only have one lifetime to get it right. You have to make the decision yourself that you have taken all you are going to take from those nasty witches/critics in your life and focus your attention on the princes/cultivators.

Begin today. Lock yourself in the bathroom and take a look in the mirror. As a child, you loved to look at your reflection. You even kissed it. You were totally accepting of yourself. Go back to that time.

Ask, "Mirror, mirror on the wall, who is the fairest of them all?" Ignore the mirror if it replies, "Step aside, I can't see who is behind you." The response you need to hear is, "You are."

Often when you look in the mirror, what passes through your

thoughts is an "I wish" list. Everybody has them: I wish I were taller; I wish I were smarter; I wish I had more money; I wish I were better looking. It's time to stop making the "I wish" list and create an "I am" list. I am me. I am extraordinary. I am special. I am God's child.

When you find out others can't accept you for who you are, don't just pretend to survive. Pretending only prevents you from getting to know and love the real, genuine, authentic you. It's easy to master the pretending game and forget who you are. There is no need to pretend any longer. It serves no purpose. It creates distances between people and renders you superficial and phony.

It's time to take off the mask that keeps people from getting close, and let them experience the warmth of you. What a shame it would be not to ever get to know you!

You have to believe you are worth knowing before you invite people inside. If you go through life always allowing others to put you down, letting people talk to you in ways that create awful feelings, your life will be one big tragedy. You won't become the person God created you to be. You'll become a doormat, allowing people to walk over and leave whatever they want in your life. The only people who appreciate doormats are people with dirty shoes.

Where Are You?

Back in 1804, a rabbi found himself spending months in a Russian czar's jail. During that time, he came to know his jail keeper a little. One day, the jail keeper said, "You're a rabbi and a wise man; me, I'm not religious at all. People are always after me to read the Bible, but I can't see what the fuss is. Here, on the very first page, God asks Adam where he is. If he's God, why doesn't he know where Adam is? One man in the whole world and God cannot find him."

The rabbi smiled and said, "God knew where Adam was. He wanted Adam to ask himself where he was." And directly to the jailer, he added, "You're forty-six years old, and you are wondering where you are."

There comes a point in all our lives when we need to wonder who we are and where we are. The self-accepting child is still within you, maybe out of sight. Call your child out of hiding. Come into the light and begin to feel good about yourself by affirming your God-given qualities that separate you from everybody else in God's world. You need to reclaim yourself, recapture the child within, and remember who you are: God's child carefully formed in God's own image. Once you forget this, you will let others say and do whatever they want. You lose respect for yourself and dismiss yourself as unimportant.

Look long and deep at your reflection and affirm your significance. Saint Augustine tells us, "We travel to wonder at the heights of mountains, at the courses of rivers, and the collection of stars at night, and we pass by ourselves and never even wonder." Do you take yourself for granted? Have you listened too long to voices of the witches and too little to the voices of the princes?

Take stock of the people around you. How do they talk to you? Do their words build you up or take you down? Are they inflators or deflators, cultivators or criticizers, princes or witches? Befriend the former and banish the latter.

Why do you let people speak to you in words that create negative feelings? What are you saying about yourself when you put up with this type of behavior? You are saying: "I don't matter." "Who cares, anyway?" "There's nothing special about me." "I am not worthy."

When you surround yourself with people who are out to sabotage you, it's hard to hear the gentle voice of God whisper to you, "Become who you are": one-of-a-kind, unique, unrepeatable, a limited edition, unlike anybody else, and terrific. As you journey inside and discover the remarkable somebody God has made you to be, turn a deaf ear to those who want to remind you you're a nobody. It has never been true.

Jesus associated with people who came from the other side of the tracks. They didn't fit in. The criticizers labeled them adulteresses, tax collectors, anonymous thieves, misfits, outcasts, beggars, whores, or just plain-run-of-the-mill sinners. When everybody else walked out, laughing, ignoring, dismissing, and judging them, Jesus, the cultivator, walked into their lives. He came to remind them to look inside themselves, where they would find treasures.

Jesus had the ability to see the hidden possibilities in every person he encountered. Jesus not only saw who a person was, but also focused on what a person could yet become, seeing not just the present reality of each person's life, but also the hidden possibilities inside. He gently stripped away all the layers of inferiority added by the critics, so everyone could see the possibilities of who they could become.

Jesus used metaphors to jog the memories of those "other side of the tracks" people, calling them "salt of the earth," "light of the world," and "the pearl of great price," images that reminded them they possessed flawless beauty. They understood they had the potential to unlock so many possibilities and see their inner beauty and worth as God's children. Once they let their lights shine, others were attracted to them. The impact was so great that lives were radically changed, each one in their own unique way. These former "losers" went out and became the spark of inspiration for others to change. Jesus cleared away all the clutter others dumped on these people, tossing aside the rubbish that had piled up from the put-downs of others.

"Eyes but do not see and ears but do not hear": this is the way Jesus introduces the message "Well, it's about time!" Jesus entered the lives of people others dismissed as unimportant, those who were morally and spiritually bankrupt—sinners, thieves, beggars, all ordinary people who just didn't believe they could do better, locked in a tower with a nasty witch blurring their vision of their real authentic selves. Jesus interrupted their lives to remind them of what they forgot—who they were: God's children, possessing intrinsic worth and value.

Once we forget who we are, all kinds of behaviors are possible. Imagine the sparkle in Jesus's eyes when a person understood and believed, "Yes, it's about time I get it together and get on living my life."

Oliver Wendell Holmes's words are good for reflection: "What lies behind us and what lies before us are small compared to what lies within us." I love the poster of the little boy, arms folded, resting his chin on them. The caption reads, "I know I'm somebody, cause God don't make junk." Well, it's about time we begin to believe it ourselves—because it is true!

Go ahead, validate and endorse your sense of dignity. Say it loud enough for all the critics to hear: "I like me. There is no one in the world like me." Once you learn to stand for yourself, you can learn to stand for anything.

Give you back to yourself. Stand up proudly and say, "I am the only me in the whole history of personkind. Isn't it great you are getting to know me?" Say it with conviction and passion. When you do, you will feel effective, lovable, productive, and capable. How you feel about yourself is based on the experiences and personal relationships you have in your life. Positive experiences and fulfilling relationships will encourage more of you to come out of the dark.

As you grow in a deep appreciation for yourself, you will accept challenges. You will become less afraid to develop your talents, willing to move out of the comfort zone and take risks. The closer you grow to knowing and loving yourself, watch and see how your life is enriched. People will want to be around you. The happiness you find in being you will become contagious. Confidence will give you the strength to become completely involved in whatever you are doing. You will be open to new ideas and insights, and remain flexible.

Better Blocker

You inherited specialness because of who you are: a uniquely created child of God. That's your identity and name. It's important for you to keep your fingers in your ears so you can't hear the voices that try to put down, criticize, or unfavorably compare to you to someone else. Father Brian Cavanaugh warns that we have to stop listening to those who say we're a nobody, an everybody, or an anybody. Then take your fingers out of your ears to hear God's voice whisper: "Become who you are—my child." Realize this: "I am a remarkable somebody!"

You enter the world with your soul branded as belonging to God. Celebrate your belonging to God as a one-of-a-kind child.

Because I am God's child, and so are you, let's grow in mutual respect, sharing together this precious dignity.

Finding a Cure for the Disease to Please

Will you look back and say, "I wish I had," or "I'm glad I did"?
Zig Ziglar

Once upon a time, a father and son and their donkey were making their way to the market. The son was sitting on the donkey as the father walked alongside. People from the crowd said, "Isn't that terrible? A young boy riding the donkey, while the old man walks. Terrible." On hearing this, the son got off the donkey and the father got on.

That man rode the donkey while the little boy walked alongside. The father overheard whispers from the crowd, saying, "Awful, that man on the donkey, while the little boy walks."

On hearing this, the father told the son to get on the donkey, too. People from the crowd said, "What a shame. Those two people on that one little donkey. Where's their consideration for the animal?"

On hearing this, they both got off and then decided to carry the donkey on their shoulders. People from the crowd said, "Now look at that. Ridiculous. Those two people carrying that heavy animal. Stupid. Why not ride it?"

The father and son never made it to the market.

Let me throw out these questions for you to think about: Are you a people pleaser? How hard is for you to say "No"? Why? Do you consistently compromise? Do you spend more time and energy on others than on yourself? Do you feel so plagued with guilt and the need for approval that you always say "Yes"? Who are you always saying "Yes" to? Why? Will they think you are thoughtless and selfish if you say "No"? Where do you fit into the relationships you have with others? Is it your own fear of getting others angry that's running your life? Are your priorities as important as everybody else's? If you bend over backwards to be assured other people's priorities come first, they evidently aren't.

If you answered, "Yes" to these questions, you're a pleaser of people. Well, it's about time you started looking at why you have the disease to please and begin looking at where you place yourself in relationship to the needs of others. Step Four in the Self-Care Solution is to realize that you are just as important as anyone else, and that your own priorities are more important to you than anyone else's.

Why shouldn't your priorities be important? Why are you the least important person in your world? Because you're a pleaser, and as a pleaser you will take a back seat to your own needs. You're only along for the ride, and you will never cause any trouble. You placate, pacify, and strive for peace at any cost. While you are easy to like, often you will over-commit yourself because you can't say "No."

Imagine the internal struggles of a pleaser. You want to say "No," but can't bring yourself to have those words fall from your lips. You bury the word inside and talk to yourself, saying, "Gosh, I could kick myself for saying 'Yes.' I already have too much to do." It's no fun. Despite all the evidence to the contrary, pleasers believe they are inadequate in everything from looks to intelligence. They have a huge need for reassurance that they are loved and appreciated. Pleasers lead their lives determined not to disturb or offend anyone. They hang up their individuality and freedom at the door, saying, "Oh, you are so much smarter than I am, you'll understand the situation better than I do." They become submissive, self-deprecating, undemanding, and apologetic, utterly lacking in self-assertion or ambition.

As a pleaser, you will acquire the self-esteem you lack through your attachments to other people. You want to be liked, so you will do whatever it takes to create and have this feeling. You're afraid of being criticized and having others disagree with you, so you will say what they want to hear, rarely putting forth your own thoughts, feelings, ideas, and opinions. You stuff them inside, creating anxiety, anger, and anguish, because you know what you really want to say, but hold back and file it away because you don't want to rock the boat and have to run the risk of someone saying, "I don't agree with that—where are you coming from?"

Just Say "No"

Well, it's about time to renovate the pleaser in you, change it, and put it away for good. Use what is called the "priority meter." When things come up, when demands are made of your time, or emergencies arise, rather than run madly about trying to do everything at once just to keep people happy, take out the priority meter and decide what must be done. Know what you can do and get it done, without feeling guilty and worrying about what everyone else is saying and thinking. Stop and ask yourself: "Are you adding more to your life than you can handle? How full is your plate? Is it so full you are overwhelmed, stressed out, and frustrated?" Remember: saying "No" isn't all that bad.

Start walking around the house for fifteen minutes in the morning and in the evening saying, "No, no, no." Get used to how nice it sounds and how great it feels. There's a wonderful sound to it. It's definite. It's final. It's no. Remember the saying, "What part of "no" don't you understand?" Say it and add nothing after to explain yourself. No is no.

When someone asks, "Hey, what do think about...?" say what you truthfully think. You have insights and opinions, so share them. People want to hear what you have to say. For too long, pleasers have held back their thoughts and feelings out of the fear of having them dismissed as ridiculous. Pleasers have played it safe and walked on eggshells out of fear of expressing what is going inside. The feelings are inside, buried, and yet waiting to come to the surface. They make an appearance every now and then. You cannot resist them forever. They will persist and come out in other behaviors, especially low self-esteem, which makes you feel you're just not good enough to express your thoughts and have others believe or accept them. So it's best to placate and give them what they want to hear.

Be a boundary setter. When you set boundaries, they will give your life shape, helping you create time for yourself, so you can say, "No" and not feel guilty. When you don't want to do something, the boundaries will help you keep your time as your time. You need to sit down and say to yourself, "These are the boundaries of my life." Promise yourself not to cross them. Keep reminding yourself to keep to the limits you have set.

In sports, when a player goes out of bounds there's a penalty, something is taken away. In the case of basketball, when you go out of bounds, you must give up the ball to the opposing team. The same will happen to you. Once you step out of bounds, there's a penalty and you'll wind up losing something. It could be your time, your peace of mind, or saying what you think and feel strongly about, but have held back.

Andy carried his anger toward his father inside himself for years. He would always say, "Yes, sir, no sir, whatever you want." He placated his father because he was afraid if he said anything wrong his father wouldn't like him. He told me, "All I ever wanted was for my father to love me and be happy with my career." So he set out to always please his father, to win his father's love. He would never express any real feelings to his father, but instead locked them inside. Once in a great while, he would let loose a sarcastic comment.

Andy was the youngest of four children. His two sisters were teachers and married with great families. His older brother was completing his training as a Navy Seal. Andy was an extremely gifted cartoon artist, yet he always felt his father thought he wasn't good enough and kind of looked down on him.

I asked him, "How do you know your father feels this way—have you asked him?"

"Oh, no," Andy said. "I just feel he does. He always brags about how great Eric is doing and how demanding it is to be a Navy Seal. Rarely have I heard any words of approval and affirmation for my work from my father."

Andy's mom always gave him overdoses of praise, hanging his cartoon panels all over the house, yet it still wasn't good enough for Andy. He needed to hear it from his father.

Andy told me he remembers his senior year in high school, when he couldn't wait to get home and show his dad his report card: all As and one C. When his dad looked at it, he asked Andy, "What's this C in physical education?" Andy told me how much that hurt him. "My dad doesn't like me," he said.

One day, his dad came home and asked if Andy had time to speak with him. Andy said, "Certainly."

His dad asked him, "Could you do me a favor?"

"Certainly."

"Well, Andy, our local Rotary Club has asked me to ask you to come and speak at our annual convention about your cartoon work—so many people from around the country read your cartoon features in their local newspapers. I told them I'd be happy to ask my son, because he's great at what he does."

"What an honor for me to do this, Dad," replied Andy.

And then he heard the words that changed his relationship, "No, Andy, what an honor for me to have you as my son and to see how you have used your God-given talents."

Andy told me, "I learned my father may not have expressed his appreciation for me, but I now feel it. Because I feel it, I am not afraid of losing it, so now we have all kinds of conversations. We argue, we joke, and we have fun together. I walked away knowing I will not lose my father's respect for me. In trying to gain his love, I tried to please my father and held back on so many occasions from saying what I wanted to say. Now I feel better about myself and less drained from all the energy I used to expend trying to please him."

As you reclaim your real, genuine, authentic self, you need to give yourself the go-ahead to say what you think without feeling guilty or afraid. The feelings you have inside are real to you. When you act contrary to what you are feeling, the real, genuine, authentic self is living in the dark and the false self is living in the light.

People pleasers stuff their feelings inside because they are afraid of hurting someone's feelings. Take the lid off and express what you are feeling at the time you are experiencing that feeling. They are neither right or wrong, moral or immoral, they simply are.

Better Blocker

The Bible has "fear not" written in it 365 times, once for each day of the year. Use "fear nots" as medicine to battle the disease to please—take one each day. Pleasers are afraid to speak out, stand up, and stick out. If anyone disagrees with them, they'll crumble, but because fear rules a pleaser's life, they will always say what others want to hear and give up their own unique thoughts and opinions.

Instead of always placating and pacifying everyone, face your fears. Turn around and look fear in the eye. Trust the voice deep within you. By bottling up your truthful thoughts and feelings, you come across as having no depth to your personality. Instead of saying, "I'm only along for the ride," get yourself into the driver's seat and take charge of your life. Stop always trying to make somebody else's day. Make it your day by discovering how good it is to think and feel for yourself without regrets and apologies.

Letting Go and Learning to Forgive

If we weren't meant to keep starting over,
would God have given us Monday?
Saying on a bumper sticker

Throughout his ministry, Jesus encountered people with the superior, arrogant attitude of trapping, labeling, and wrongly judging others. Remember the scene in John's gospel (8:1–11), of the woman caught in the act of adultery? After hearing the accusation and the punishment, think about Jesus's response: he bends down and scribbles in the sand all her past shortcomings. But then he erases them, letting them all blow away. He was probably thinking, "They just don't get it. It's about second chances, changing and growing. It's about conversion, not condemning, about the present and not the past, about forgiving, not fault finding."

Well, it's about time to let go of the past. Step Five in the Self-Care Solution is to learn to finish each day and put it behind you, to forgive and forget.

Everybody has a past. You know you can never change it, but only the amount of attention you will give it, the time you want to live in it, and the hold it has on you. You also know there are people who want to circle the wagons around you, and trap you in what was. They want to accuse you and call you names as they pick up a stone to fling at you, reminding you of your past behavior.

Your past can be laced with responsibilities, blunders, poor decisions, actions you aren't proud of, words you wish you had never expressed, mistakes you made, failed relationships, addictions, or hurts.

Some people will never let you forget your past, and will use it to keep you from growing, changing, and doing better. They like to begin by asking, "Hey, remember when you did this?" Of course you do. Yet your response to them depends on your acceptance of your past, your ownership of what you did and how you improved yourself. When people pose this question, they aren't looking for a response but a reaction. They know what button they have pushed, secretly pleased they have one over on you, and they just can't wait for your response.

When someone asks if you remember a past misdeed, just say "yes" and stop there. Anything that follows the "yes" is a defense or explanation. "Yes" will disarm them, leaving them nothing more to say than, "Oh, okay." Remain cool and calm, and don't let people open the wounds you have worked hard to mend. Give a quiet and gentle, yet loud and firm, "Yes." Indicate you have accepted what you did, made the adjustments for the better, and improved yourself—now you want to put away the past, because it is powerless and useless. You belong to the *now*, not the *was*.

Face the Past

When you face the past, you grow out of denial and toward ownership. Look at the baggage you have been carrying around, the way you have dealt with situations that didn't turn out for the best, and the people in your life who want to continually mark you as a loser. The past weighs you and limits you from being fully mindful of the present.

Face it. Open up the baggage and look through it. It's part of your history. Take it out of hiding and examine it. See it for what it is: stuff that is over and done with. Sure, you can ignore the past, but it is still there. Once you come to terms with it, it has no more power over you. It can't burden you any longer.

Face it. Listen to your heart and your feelings. Express them out loud. You may be carrying around a belly full of anger, anxiety, embarrassment, fear, worry, and more. It's time to let these feelings loose and integrate them into your life. The past is who you were, not who you are.

Face it. You know you have claimed your past when you integrate the past into who you are as a growing person. Who you were, with positive changes, brings you to who you are at this time in your life.

At this point, you need to trust that after you create new goals, correct behaviors, and develop healthier habits, the past will have no more power over you than what you give it. If you keep conjuring it up inside yourself, it will run the show of your life. Find the courage to let it evaporate and disappear. Keep your eyes and ears open for the new possibilities that will show themselves as you move on.

After you look at what went wrong, you can begin to replace the past with what you need in your life, what you need to become your authentic self, living connected to others in healthy relationships.

Replace the past by healing a hurt you've been carrying around, an anger you have toward a parent, spouse, child, or friend, making better decisions, settling unfinished business, and relating maturely. Name the behaviors you aren't happy with, and examine what has motivated these behaviors. Get inside the unhealthy habits that may have turned your life upside down, and go after the inner strength you need to renovate them into healthy habits.

After you face the past and replace it, erase it. Forget about it. It is settled, removed, and forgiven. Read Philippians, Chapter 3:13–14, which begins with Paul's autobiography. He had a past he wasn't bragging about, yet he gives us a simple instruction on how to deal with it. He sums it all up when he writes: "Forget what lies behind, but move forward to what lies ahead." It's called spiritual amnesia—develop it. The past now serves no purpose other than to offer lessons for the future and chances to change your performance by living rightly now and not repeating your history. Write it new.

Obsessing over your past takes from you all the energy you need to focus on living fully in the now. Your past brings you to where you are at this time; that is all. See it as a teacher who is concerned about your learning, improving, and doing better this time.

When you decide to live in your past, giving people the power to bring it up in every conversation, your life will be filled with two things: guilt and anxiety. Once you have these two "gifts" in your life, they like to hang around a long time and keep giving to you more and more. Don't do it. Separate yourself from the past and from people who won't let it go.

Everyone has excavators, people in their lives who cannot free themselves from what we did in the past. They just can't let it die. They hold on to it as if it has some security. They see you as a result of what you did or didn't do. They like to go out of their way to bring it up, creating feelings of blame.

When you see these people coming, don't run away. Stand firm. When they want to push you beyond your "Yes," ask them: "Have you ever heard the wise old saying, 'never fall over what's behind you'? It's good advice because if you live in your past you are forever falling over something behind you." Tell them, "That's who I was, carrying around baggage from yesterday and falling all over it, but now it's part of my history, and it isn't who I am at this moment. Sit down and let me share my conversion with you, so you'll get to know the real me, and you won't need to keep digging up what I have done and have dealt with." They won't bring up the past again.

People who always want to dig up the past and dump it on you just don't get it. More importantly, they don't understand this is not who you are at this moment; you have changed and grown. But they can't see it, because they don't want to. They want to see you as a product of your past and use it to keep you in place—and you know what that's called, don't you? Control. Don't waste precious time trying to explain it to them. Tell them to get out of your way as you move forward, not backward.

You decide what you are going to do with the excavators in your life. Don't back away—stand up to those who want to keep a scorecard of harm, mistakes, and failures from your past. Look them right in the eye and say, "Let those who have no past be the first to throw a stone at me. Be my guest." One by one, they will walk away.

Well, it's about time to ask yourself: "Are you going to keep beating yourself up with your past or let it die? Are you going to still cling to the past and have it rule you?" There's no better way to waste the present moment than to dwell on the past. The past is over. You belong to the present. You have never seen or experienced today before, so live it.

It is time to ask what you can do right, not mourn what you did wrong. You are more than your yesterdays. Who you are right now is all you need to be. Continually look inside changing, resolving and removing all obstacles from your history so you can see the richness of your God-given self.

Learn to Forgive

A teacher once told her students to bring a clear plastic bag and a sack of potatoes to school. For every person they had refused to forgive, they were to choose a potato, write on it the name and date, and put it in the plastic bag. Some of their bags were quite heavy.

They were then told to carry this bag with them everywhere for one week, putting it beside their bed at night, on the car seat when driving, next to their desk at school. Lugging this sack of potatoes around made it clear what a weight the students carried spiritually when they chose not to forgive. They had to pay attention to the bag all the time so they wouldn't forget it and keep leaving it in embarrassing places. Naturally, the condition of the potatoes deteriorated to a nasty smelly slime.

This tale is a wonderful metaphor to remember as you continue to renovate yourself. It's an effective image for the price we pay to keep alive. Too often, we think of forgiveness as a gift to the other person. It is, but it's also a gift for ourselves.

When a friend is angry with someone, just mention the word "forgive," and listen to your friend's response: "Forgive her? Right!" or "After what he's done to me, no way will I forgive him!" But learning to forgive is an essential step in accepting the past and moving on from it.

You keep spiritually fit by clearing clutter, capturing your intrinsic worth, concentrating on the present, creating your own priorities, and celebrating forgiveness.

I share this with permission: Ray told me that since their divorce, his wife tried everything to keep him from seeing their children. "I was wrong," he said, "But she's still bitter." Ray told his ex-wife, "I'm sorry, you didn't deserve it." What else could he do? He couldn't erase the past, only change, grow, and do better.

Tina Turner sings it well, "Holding on to the past only stands in our way." It does. Believe it. It starves our relationships by depriving them of warmth, care, love, closeness, and compassion.

Hurts are caused by thoughtless acts, harsh words, poor choices, and unfair criticisms—all sins—which disrupt your life and harm your relationships. Let's be truthful. The last time someone hurt you, wronged you, or took something that belonged to you, did you feel like saying, "Don't worry about it" or did you feel like getting even?

The latter is normal and natural. You see yourself as the innocent, so justice is accomplished when you hurt those who damaged you: "an eye for an eye." Now the slate is clean and our pain is gone. But is it? Many who seek revenge find it's not "sweet," but "sour," leaving you isolated and unhappy.

Too often, forgiveness is confused with approval. There is a difference. While you can never approve of a hurt or a damage that has been done, you can forgive. You can only have peace in your life and mended relationships when you say, "I'm sorry. I messed up. Forgive me."

Holding on to past anger by punishing people holds back love, warmth, and compassion. Saint Paul mentions what happens when you choose to not forgive: "hatreds, rivalry, outbursts of anger, selfishness, dissension, and factions" (Galatians 5:20–21) will fill your life.

How long will you keep building fences of bitterness, anger, hatred, revenge, and resentment? How long will you continue fighting the cold war of silence, judging, condemning, and avoiding? The early church knew what to do with negative feelings and actions when hurt: "get rid of bitterness, anger, shouting, slander, along with all malice— be kind to one another, compassionate and forgiving each other" (Ephesians 4:31–32). Remember, the grave is too late to forgive.

Finding no room in your heart to forgive is like grabbing a rattlesnake by the tail: you're going to be bitten. As the venom of bitterness works its way through your body, a death will occur that is worse than physical death; it has the potential to turn you into a person you will dislike, possibly destroying those around you.

Unforgiving people have pebbles in their shoes, preventing them from walking in Jesus's spirit of second chances. By withholding patience, kindness, gentleness, and understanding, the unforgiving person is trapped. A person unable to forgive always loses. Regardless of how wrong the other person may have been, refusing to forgive means the other person owns you and your life will be miserable.

Rush Forward into Forgiveness

Well, it's about time to soften your heart. We hear these words at Mass: "Your spirit changes our hearts: Enemies begin to speak to one another, those estranged join hands in friendship" (Preface: Eucharistic Prayer II for Reconciliation). It's time to look inside your heart and give up grudges, bitterness, and retribution, and let God's "spirit work so understanding puts an end to strife, hatred is quenched by mercy and vengeance gives way to forgiveness" (*Preface: Eucharistic Prayer II for Reconciliation*).

Ask yourself, "Do I want to waste precious time and energy carrying these nasty feelings?" If not, give them up and forgive. If possible, sit down and talk with the person who wronged you. Share your feelings, listen to each other without interrupting, and then forgive each other. Healing a relationship doesn't necessarily mean it will be like it was before, but now negative feelings are resolved and released.

Charlie came to see me about a problem he was having. He was angry with his father for dying. He said, "He died just when I was getting to know him as a friend, a buddy. We'd fish, hunt, and golf together. Now it's all gone."

I told him, "You have unfinished business with your father. Go and tell him."

"He's dead," Charlie said, "How can I?"

I said, "Get in your car and go to the cemetery and tell him how angry you are with him." He left my office looking confused.

Two weeks later, Charlie came in and told me, "I feel better. I let it out. I gave it to him. I got into my car and made the trip to Philadelphia and stood over his grave and blasted him. Then I stopped and closed my eyes and said to myself what I felt he would respond. Wow, I never realized how much energy keeping all that anger inside can do to a person."

I agreed and applauded Charlie for what he did.

Forgiveness brings healing, freedom, and peace back into our lives. It opens our eyes so we can see what happened. One day, the roles of wronged and wrongdoer may be reversed.

One of my favorite gospel stories is Luke's parable of the prodigal son (Luke 15:11–32). It was the son's memory of his father's goodness that changed his heart, enabling the son to return home and ask to be forgiven. The son isn't the hero. It's the father—the one hurt—who enables the son to get his life together and go home. A powerful action we overlook is this: "He ran to his son, embraced him and kissed him" (Luke 15:20). It's not the custom of elder men to run; this action shows the one wronged moves first to forgive.

Our God is calling us on our journey to break the cycle of bitterness, anger, resentment, hurt, and retaliation. Take the first step: forgive those who have harmed you, embrace them, and never look back.

Every Sunday, Sarah tells Father Jim that she talks to Jesus and that Jesus tells her all kinds of things. One Sunday, the Father said to Sarah, "Tonight when you talk to Jesus, ask him what sins I confessed."

Sarah replied, "Okay."

The following Sunday, Father Jim inquired, "Well, did you ask Jesus?"

"Yes," Sarah said. "He said he forgot."

You cannot forget what hurt was done to you until you begin to forgive. Until you do, bitterness, hatred, resentment, revenge, and anger control your life. These feelings harden your heart.

Cast out the Reminder Demon who wants you to keep the cold war going and build the walls higher. Let it die, giving you a soft heart and changing you into a better person.

Your heart is like a pecan, covered with a hard shell that holds sweet (forgiveness) and bitter (nasty feelings) parts within. Use the renovation of you as a time to dissolve the outer shell and let Jesus inside to help remove the bitter part, so you can embrace forgiveness. You can let the bitterness destroy you or you can allow Jesus to recreate you into the person he wants you to be, healer and forgiver. That's how you care for yourself.

Well, it's about time to fence-mend with spouses, parents, children, family, and all those you feel wronged you. It's time to make your life and relationships healthy. Take those nasty feelings out of the darkness and bring them into the light; dump them into the garbage so your life and relationships can be made whole again.

Say this prayer: "Lord, I choose to forgive (name that person) for (what they did) even though I feel (share the painful feelings). Lord, I choose not to hold any grudges against (name) any longer. Thank you, Lord, for freeing me from my bitterness toward (name). Keep (name) safe in your love. Amen."

Better Blocker

Perhaps you have heard of the little boy who prayed, "Father, forgive us our trespasses, as we give it to those who trespass against us."

The little boy was honest. So many times you want to lash back instead of forgive back. Lewis Smedes, author of *Forgive and Forget: Healing the Hurts We Don't Deserve*, writes: "Forgiveness is spiritual surgery. You slice out of your past damage that shouldn't be there."

When you don't, it comes back to you. I call it the "boomerang effect." When you throw out revenge, unkind words, or nastiness, they all return to you.

Jesus encourages you to be compassionate forgivers. When words have been exchanged, damaging the relationship, follow Jesus and go out and be the first to settle the wrong and heal the hurt. It's surrendering your right to get even.

Forgiveness frees you from bitterness and resentment. You don't rub it in, you rub it out and then have peace in your life.

Connecting with Each Other

When you have people in your life, it makes up for all you don't have.
Ann Landers

A UPS driver pulled up to a country house and noticed an elderly gentleman on his hands and knees, planting flowers, while his wife sat on the porch rocking back and forth. As the gentleman planted flowers, he whistled. The UPS driver couldn't recognize the tune the old man was whistling, so as he approached with the package, he asked: "Sir, what song are you whistling?"

"None in particular," the man replied. "You see, that's my wife on the porch and we've been married for fifty-eight years. Two years ago, she lost her sight. Since then, she's afraid to be left alone. So whenever I'm not sitting next to her, I whistle, so she won't feel afraid, but safe."

As we stop and think about what we live for and what matters in our lives, we usually think of some person: a spouse, child, parent, or friend. To thrive and survive, we need warmhearted contact with other people. We need to feel we are connected.

Just as our bodies have a need for air and food, our souls have a need to connect with other people. We are at our best when we are connected in working relationships with another person, and at our worst when we are disconnected. Without feeling connected, we can't grow into a full human person. Step 6 in the Self-Care Solution is learning how to connect with other people so we can feed our own souls.

Read Antione de Saint-Exupéry's *The Little Prince*, a powerful little book about relationships. The Prince is searching the universe for friendship. When he encounters the fox, he learns much about getting along. The fox tells him, "Life is about establishing ties. Once the ties are established, we become responsible." The Prince knows the great care he has given to his beloved rose, back on his planet. He protects it by keeping it under a glass dome. He watches out for it so the insects don't kill it. He realizes the uniqueness in his rose. He has a connection. He has formed a relationship with another being, one he is now responsible for. That feeling of responsibility makes his soul feel complete.

When we invite another person into our lives and we connect by establishing a tie with them, then we become responsible for each other. We need to look out and be there for each other.

The close-to-the-vest, standoffish life is bad for our bodies and souls. Like a vitamin deficiency, we experience a human contact deficiency, which weakens the body and soul. Just as we need vitamin C each day, we also need heavy doses of positive human contact, which give us energy and connect us with each other on an intimate emotional level so we don't die from loneliness.

An elderly man in Phoenix called his son in New York, saying: "I hate to ruin your day, but I have to tell you that your mother and I are divorcing; forty-five years of misery is enough."

"Pop, what are you taking about?" the son shouted in surprise.

"We can't stand the sight of each other any longer," the old man said. "We're sick of each other, and I'm sick of talking about this, so you call your sister in Chicago and tell her," and he hung up.

Upset, the son called his sister, who couldn't believe what she was hearing. "What, they're getting a divorce? I'll take care of this," she shouted.

She called Phoenix and said, "Daddy, you're not getting divorced. Don't do a thing until I get there. I'm calling my brother back, and we'll both be there tomorrow," and hung up.

The old man hung up his phone, too, and turned to his wife. "Okay, they're coming for Thanksgiving. You think of something for Christmas."

This anecdote illustrates a unique way to remind those we need in our lives to stop neglecting us and start paying attention to us.

Well, it's about time we take heavy doses of vitamin C—we need to connect, communicate, create, and care.

Vitamin C: Connect

As we get our insides in order, we discover our souls don't hunger for power, paychecks, popularity, prestige, and pleasure. Our souls hunger to be connected, to belong to another person. It's our basic need: to love and be loved, and feel as though we matter to somebody.

Connections with another person give us the freedom to be open with them. When we invite them inside and share who we are with them, we believe we will be accepted and loved. We believe the people we love will always be there. We tend to put off saying and showing love until tomorrow—but eventually, there will be no more tomorrows.

I know people who live with regrets because they took another person for granted and missed opportunities to connect, express, and demonstrate affection. Well, it's about time we say it, "I love you"; and show it with hugs and kisses. When we fail to connect through words and gestures, the relationship slowly dies. Connecting with each other lifts us up and gives us life, but it needs to be demonstrated. We aren't mind readers.

A husband and wife went to see a therapist to save their marriage. After about thirty minutes, the therapist got up and gave the wife a big hug. He said to the husband, "Your wife needs this every day."

The husband responded, "Okay, doctor, I can bring her in here every Monday and Friday."

A joke, but one that contains a nugget of truth. Foreigner sums it up best when they sing, "I want to know what love is. I want you to show me. I want to feel what love is. I know you can show me."

After twenty years as a priest, I have never read the obituary of a person who died from an overdose of love and care, forgiveness and compassion, hugs and kisses. Life is about belonging to each other. It's about being connected to each other and having that one person in our lives who will be there when everybody else walks away.

During my ministry, I've lost track of the number of people who have told me: "All I ever wanted to hear was 'I love you.'" I have seen people wait for an apology or visit that will bring them peace before they die.

Jim was burying his wife of twenty-two years. As they were leaving the cemetery, he hugged her casket and said, "Father, I loved my wife."

The priest responded, "I know you did. Let's go home, Jim."

A second time, he repeated those words, "Father, I loved my wife."

"Jim, I know and she loved you, it's time to leave," the priest said.

Then Jim said, "Father, I loved my wife and one day I almost told her I did."

Too often, we only realize the value of a person once they are dead. We don't know what we have until it's gone. Death teaches us we don't have forever to say it and show it: "I love you." It shouldn't take a tragedy to open our eyes and see what we have. It's hard to play catch-up for all the valuable and rich moments of love we let slip away by putting them off. Ask yourself: "Who are the people in my life I have been taking for granted?" "Who do I need to reconnect with now?" Then do something about it—a visit, a hug, a kiss, a telephone call, expressing how important the other person is to you. That's making a solid connection and keeping it together.

Charity begins at home, so begin with gestures of attention by doing things together, showing interest in one another, and making each other a priority. The prophet Isaiah says, "Don't turn your back on your own" (58:7).

Vitamin C: Communicate

One of the biggest mistakes we make in life is underestimating the power of communication. We simply take for granted that communication really is a skill, and that it can help "make or break" our connections with each other. Once we open up our lives and share what's going on inside, and feel there is a connection with the other person, that's communication. It is the number one quality for keeping a healthy relationship growing better.

When we communicate, we feel as though the other person understands us and is taking us seriously. Have we lost this today? Are we going in so many different directions that we don't take the time to communicate with each other, except through e-mail, voice-mail, or Post-It notes? If we want to stay connected in a meaningful way, we have to slow down and talk to each other. We need to practice eye-to-eye communication, getting inside each other's worlds, listening, talking, laughing, crying, and enjoying, going to that special place where we can share our inner feelings, thoughts, fantasies, hurts, dreams, complaints, failures, and successes, without holding back, without the fear that we will be condemned, attacked, or lectured.

Often, we may pollute our communication with trivializing buzzwords. They stop the conversation: "Oh, puh-leeze," "Don't go there," "Same old, same old," "Whatever," "Yadda, yadda, yadda," or "Been there, done that." These expressions cut off the other person, communicating that you aren't concerned about what the other person wants to express. They prevent any real human connecting and interacting. It's like saying, "I have better things to do, and this bores me." Communicating is about listening, responding, revealing, and engaging with another person. It's not shutting them down or cutting them off.

The only way we can get to know each other inside and out is by talking with each other. Once we do, we will reveal who we are and what we are all about. It's self-disclosure. It's taking the risk and saying, "Come inside." When the other person does, then we gradually shed all those layers that have kept our real, genuine, authentic selves hidden. I'd like to suggest my five levels of communication.

Level one: could care less. At this level, it's, "Don't get in my face; I don't want to hear anything you want to say after I ask how you are. That's where it stops. That's all I want to know." This is the safest and weakest of all the levels of communication. It's the kind of talk we hear at parties, just to be social. There is no desire to get involved in another person's life.

Level two: keep it simple. "I don't want to hear what you think or feel. Just tell me the facts." Remember *Dragnet*, the television show where Sergeant Joe Friday would say, "Just the facts, ma'am"? Anything beyond that isn't appreciated or welcomed.

At this level of communication, nothing is disclosed or revealed about us as a thinking-feeling person. This attitude prevents us from having any sincere, open communication connection with each other. Boundaries are enforced and shields are activated, telling us, "This is as far we go."

When our communication bounces between levels one and two, it is just surface talk and we will know nothing more. Our relationships with each other will be one-dimensional and superficial. In some cases, such as a short elevator ride with strangers, levels one and two are fine. With your spouse or friend, you need to move deeper.

Level three: tell me more. When we communicate at this level, we feel encouraged to share our thoughts, ideas, opinions, and positions, because we will not be criticized for them or told, "You can't think that way in this house or have that idea in this relationship." This is when we approach the water and test it by first putting in a toe. Once we say what we think and the other person nods and says, "Good thought. Great insight," we keep the lines of communication open and want to reveal more. The other person doesn't have to agree with us, but just be open to all the possibilities of looking at an issue, a situation, or a problem through our eyes.

Level four: going deeper. We've tested the waters and discovered it's safe to jump in, so we want to go deeper and add our feelings to our thoughts in the conversation. We find out the other person isn't going to trample on our ideas or dismiss them as ridiculous. The other person listens and then responds to what we are sharing with them. This level is important for quality and richness in our relationships. It's when we add heart and guts to it all. Our feelings tell us we are alive. They aren't either right or wrong, they simply are.

When our communication reaches levels three and four, it becomes possible for us to experience true intimacy in our relationships. At these levels, we begin self-disclosure by exposing our ideas and feelings, our thoughts and convictions, to another person. When we open ourselves up and put out our opinions and discuss what we cherish and value, the other person's reactions and responses determine if we will continue to reveal more and more. If we are cast aside, not taken seriously, and laughed at, we will shut down and retreat back into ourselves by playing it safe or saying what the other person wants to hear. But when we are encouraged to tell more and go deeper, we move to our final level of communication.

When people communicate with each other at levels three and four, they will reveal their deepest thoughts, ambitions, and concerns. When we listen, we will pick up on these subtle, underlying issues that are always there, the unspoken emotions and concerns. And when we "hear" them and empathize with them (either verbally or nonverbally), the speaker often remarks, "Boy, you really know how I feel," or, "Gee, you really understand exactly what's going on with me." When we feel that sense of comfort, we feel safe to move on to the next level of communication.

Level five: right on. We have made an intimate connection. I once heard intimacy defined as "into me you see." That's great. We become transparent to each other. It's getting inside each other's worlds and accepting our thoughts and endorsing our feelings; it's liking what we are experiencing. The other person understands and empathizes with us. We are in harmony with each other. It's a blending of what we think and feel, encouraging us to keep going deeper.

During a high-school retreat, I asked the seniors, "What moment in your life do you wish had never come to an end?" Amanda said, "About five months ago, my mom and I went shopping and then to dinner. We just sat and talked for three hours. It was great."

We need to give to each other our full, undivided attention. It's not only about talking, but also about listening to the other person's point of view and to their feelings. There's an Irish saying, "God gave us two ears and one mouth, so we talk less and listen more." Listening means I focus on you and remove all that will distract us. Stop worrying about grabbing the cell phone, powering up the laptop, or retrieving voice mail. Listen. Hear the words behind the words, the feelings that need to be expressed.

We all need to develop better listening skills. It's very hard to be a good listener—at any level—if we're not fully attending to what others are saying and feeling. Much of the time when people are speaking to us, our heads become filled with our own personal thoughts and agendas: thinking how we're going to respond, thinking negative thoughts about the other person, thinking how we would think or feel in a similar situation.

Often, when we talk with another person our own conversations are taking place our inside our heads. We are thinking of what we are going to say next, a rebuttal, a way to disarm the speaker or put them in their place if we are being confronted. If they come to talk with us because something is bothering them, we want to quickly solve their problem. It's the internal-strategy dialogue we have with ourselves, "What do I say next? What quick answer can I give? What would I do?" We tell them how they should feel or not feel.

When we respond this way, we are not listening, just looking for a quick solution to an uncomfortable situation. Allowing the other person to talk, getting it all out, will help them feel better. Stop looking for a quick solution. Sit there, relax, and listen. Hand them a tissue if they cry.

We want to play the role of Mr. and Mrs. Fix-it-all, but to listen well we must put these thoughts aside and be with the other person. We've got to fully attend to their words and inner emotions. We've got to actively work to put ourselves in their shoes and listen to them speak. And we've got to keep an open mind to discover the value or merit in whatever the other person says, giving them the space to work through it on their own with our support and encouragement, instead of putting our thoughts and feelings into their heads and hearts.

Look out for these blocks to listening: mind reading, rehearsing, filtering, judging, daydreaming, advising, sparring, being right, changing the subject, and placating. When you feel yourself doing any of these negative actions, stop immediately and return to active listening mode.

When we don't listen to each other, the results are usually frustration, anger, misunderstanding, and hurt. Listening is a learned skill. If a person is raised in an environment where people don't listen and can't express their feelings, they will bring this into their relationships. However, the good news is that we can change the habit of being shallow listeners.

When a relationship is wounded, it can only be healed with good communication. True attentive and reflective listening offers the opportunity for others to share their life with us. Listening gives you the chance to heal hurts and build bridges in a relationship. When someone listens to us and we feel understood, we are much more likely to trust the other person, thus opening the gate for more intimate communication.

We may think, "What is so important about listening? I listen!" Sure we do. But how? How adept are we, for example, in getting people to come right out and really talk to us? Before we can get the most out of a listening situation, others must first believe that we really want to listen. They must feel that when they tell us something, it will be received by us in the proper spirit. Learn to listen beyond the words, with your heart as well as your ears. Observe the signs of the inner feelings such as voice quality, facial expressions, body posture, and motions. These actions are revealing and sometimes may have an opposite meaning from the spoken word. A friend put it this way: "You listened as if you wanted to hear what I was going to say, as if it was really important to you. And that makes me feel good!"

I've sat with couples after a breakup, who say, "If I only knew the real reason she/he left me, I could get on with my life." Mamma's advice: "No matter how bad it is, tell me the truth." Too often in our relationships we can be honest, but not truthful. Honesty is the tip of the iceberg, while truthfulness is the iceberg itself. We keep it hidden from each other because we don't have the courage to express what we truthfully feel. We owe it to each other to tell the truth in our relationships. Relationships will only grow when we tell the absolute complete truth to each other, holding nothing back.

Confronting each other in a hurting relationship is not a bad thing; it's required. Confrontation means, "I care enough about this relationship to sit down and talk truthfully and stop playing games, pretending everything is fine when it's coming apart. We have to get everything out of the closet, all the baggage we are carrying, together with unresolved issues and repressed feelings, and talk about what is going on in our lives." This isn't just self-care; it's other-care. It's being concerned about us as a people, connected to each other in this relationship.

When people sit down knee to knee and speak the truth about their relationships, the possibility exists for reconnecting and reconciling. If people keep everything inside and resist bringing it out in truthful communication, the relationship is headed for the graveyard.

Connect and communicate with those who matter: spouses, children, parents, and friends. Mike Rutherford, from Mike and the Mechanics, sings, "I wish I could have told him in the living years. It's too late when we die to admit we didn't see eye to eye." It's okay to get in each other's face. You don't have to agree with everything, just talk and listen. Be open to each other's point of view. How much do you know about your kids? Sit down and talk. Who are their friends? What are they reading? How about their kind of music? What do you know about it? Find out. How much do your kids know about you? Connect and communicate with each other.

I recall a great book I saw at a booksellers' convention a few years ago, called, *Dad Was Quite the Guy and Mom Was Quite the Gal*. The book was filled with questions and statements: "What three words do you want to be remembered by when you die? What's your favorite food? Who are your heroes? Write down the color of your eyes. Talk about your first date." Mom and Dad take time to fill it in and when their child gets married they give it to them. What you're saying is "I have time for you, because you're important to me."

Mother Teresa warns, "Everybody today seems to be in a hurry. No one has time to give to others; children to their parents, parents to their children, spouses to each other." We have to slow down and create time to be with one another, or the moment will pass us by.

Vitamin C: Create
The Orthodox Jews have a wonderful observance. From sundown Friday to sundown Saturday they cannot do any work. They can't drive, talk on the telephone, or go shopping. On that day they connect with each other. They communicate with their neighbors and friends. Their religion forces them to make time to connect and communicate with one another and their God because it's so essential for quality living.

Today we have too many distractions. Our lives are cluttered with one appointment or activity after another. All of this keeps us from focusing on what is important. Do you want your tombstone to read:

"Here lies Mary Smith? She returned every e-mail, attended every company meeting, made every business trip, and yet missed three of her daughter's school plays and twelve anniversary dinners with her husband"? Turn off the TV, put down the newspaper, clear the calendar, and create blocks of time for just hanging out with each other.

I knew a couple, Sam and Rose, whose lives were filled with so much that they felt they were growing apart in their relationship. As Christmas approached, they decided that instead of giving each other material gifts, they would give the gift of time. So they gave each other Wednesday. This day would be just for them.

After having breakfast, they'd do things together for the rest of the day, blocking out all their concerns about the work that needed to be done or the messages on the telephone. Everything would still be there the next day, when they returned to work. Their day was filled with complete and exclusive attention to each other. By creating this unique solution, Sam and Rose were able to work on their relationship, ensuring they grew together, not apart.

Moments of paying attention to each other are unrepeatable and unforgettable. We need more of them, now. Tomorrow may be too late. Well, it's about T-I-M-E:

- (T)alking and listening are ways to stay close to each other. Sitting down and sharing stories of joys, hurts, opinions, disappointments, and faith will keep you connected.
- (I)nvolving yourself in each other's activities at school, church, or work expresses, "I'm interested in you."
- (M)aking it a priority to come together as family one day or evening during the week says, "You're essential."
- (E)njoying the time you spend together will fill your heart with rich and lasting memories.

Relationships take work and need caring. But when you take the time to nurture your relationships, you create love and intimacy, which deepens love, and quality time, which keeps love growing. Without love, our relationships slowly die.

Leo Buscaglia, author and teacher, was asked to judge a contest to find the most caring child. The winner was a four-year-old boy who went next door to visit an elderly gentleman whose wife had recently died. When his mother asked him what he had said to their neighbor, the little boy said, "Nothing, mommy. I just climbed onto his lap, sat there, and helped him cry."

The elderly neighbor connected with the little boy, communicating because this child had created the time to notice another person in need. Through the simple act of caring, the potential exists to turn around whatever life gives to us, good or bad. We will get much more out of life when we let others into our lives.

Vitamin C: Caring

We need more caring in our world, people who reach out to connect, communicate, and create time. John Paul II tells us, "Almsgiving, far from being reduced to an occasional offering of money, means an attitude of sharing...open your eyes to see beside you so many brothers and sisters who have needs" (*L'Osservatore Romano*, February 17, 1997).

We cannot place a value on sitting with a person who is lonely or dying, listening to a friend who is upset or afraid, or spending time with a relative or neighbor who is hospitalized or housebound. If you haven't done any of these things, start now. Caring through gestures of kind acts continues when we forget and focus, find and fill.

Forget the excuses, especially the big three: how, where, and when. Often you hear: "But I don't know how to help." It doesn't take advanced degrees or special talents to help others, just a desire to respond to God's call to help each other. Ask your parish priest, call your local hospital, soup kitchen, jail, or nursing home to inquire: Where can I help? How can I help? What can I do? Forget the weakest excuse: "Sorry, no time." Make it. We have time for so many other things. Clear your schedule one day or evening a week or a month for a few hours to make acts of charity a priority. If you want to do something, you'll find the time.

Focus on what you can do and believe in your God-given ability to bring joy into a person's life. Small gestures will say, "I care about you": bake cookies or bread; give the favor of light housework or a ride for an appointment, help out at a soup kitchen, clothing and food bank, or local shelter; check on a friend who's going through a difficult time.

Find and fill a need. A simple act of kindness will make another person's life easier: raking yards, trimming shrubs, mowing the grass, or shoveling the snow. Begin with something you feel comfortable doing. Read a story to a person. Help write a card or a letter for a person crippled with arthritis. Pray the rosary with guests at a nursing home. Works of charity will touch people's hearts: plant flowers, clean up the church pews after Mass, baby sit, take someone to lunch or grocery shopping with you. Reaching out with friends and family together can be exciting. Stay with it and it will become a way of life.

There are many ways we can "serve each other in love" (Galatians 5:13). Our spiritual growth depends upon our willingness to extend ourselves by connecting and participating in people's lives. It might be overused, but it's true: "Love isn't love 'til it's given away" (Oscar Hammerstein II). Our acts of charity make God's love real, flowing through us to others, as his instruments of care.

Kind and caring gestures, done without expecting anything in return, will make our lives complete and our spiritual lives enriched because, "Your Father who sees what you do in secret will repay you" (Matthew 6:4).

Read Phillip McGraw's book, *Life Strategies*. As I was reflecting on this chapter, I came across this thought: "If you want to take purposeful actions in life, I would suggest a time-honored formula: Be. Do. Have." This relates to gestures of kindness, charity, and care:

- *Be* committed to reaching out in loving acts to those in need.
- *Do* whatever it takes to lift someone's cross, making their lives easier.
- *Have* an exciting, rich and meaningful life.

Do is always the hardest. We hear, "If I had only known, I would have helped you." Or, "Why didn't you call me?" Well, it's about time we embrace the opportunity to allow Jesus to use us to do something beautiful for our brothers and sisters by finding a need, filling it, and watching the difference it makes.

Take the time and read James 2:14–26. He is correct: Faith without deeds (acts of kindness, charity, and care) is of no value. There is something for each of us to do: we become true disciples of Jesus at the moment we reach out to connect, communicate, create, and care with another person.

Our God is not an absentee God, creating us, and then disappearing from our lives. God promises: "I will never forget you" (Isaiah 49:15). God wants to intimately connect with us. We belong to him. "I have redeemed you; I have called you by name; you are mine" (Isaiah 43:1). Jesus reminds us, "I call you friend" (John 15:15). Jesus understands the feelings expressed in these words, "You're not one of our kind," or "Go back where you belong." Jesus steps into our lives and wonders: "Is everybody leaving and forgetting about you? Not me. I'm here, to stay, there's room in my life for you." Jesus is there to connect, communicate, and create the time for us.

Better Blocker

> Henry and Agatha were married for sixty-eight years. A reporter took Henry aside and said, "I'm impressed, Henry, that after all these years you still refer to your wife as 'sweetheart, honey, and dear.'"
>
> Henry bent over and whispered into the reporter's ear saying, "To tell the truth, I forgot her name two years ago."

To keep love alive and the relationship on track, care, share, and play fair. When you care for the other people in your life you're saying, "I'm concerned about you and don't want you to be neglected from a lack of attention." Caring people watch out for each other, in good times and bad, enabling the other to take one more step. They behave responsibly with their words and actions.

Our caring relationships only stay connected through dialogue, not two parallel monologues. Listen more and talk less. Take your cue from nature: your ears aren't meant to be shut, but your mouth is. Listen and silent are spelled with the same letters. Do you think there's a connection? Listening is giving the other person the attention with the intention to understand them. Stop if you are having trouble communicating with a spouse, child, or parent, from giving advice or lecturing. Nobody cares how much you know unless they know how much you care. A favorite motto of mine is, "Talking is sharing, and listening is caring." Sharing and caring happen by swapping stories, sharing struggles and exchanging laughter.

Finally play fair. Never let the sun go down on your anger. Try to work it out before you go to bed. Reconciling, healing, and forgiving help you play fair. These words are important to say: "I'm sorry," as well as these: "I know you are, I accept it."

STEP 7

Casting Away Heartache

I give myself a good cry if I need it.
But then I concentrate on the good things still in my life.
Morrie Schwartz,
from *Tuesdays with Morrie* (Mitch Albom)

Jacob was about to begin the biggest battle of his life. At seven years old, he had been diagnosed with leukemia. With immediate treatment, Jacob's leukemia went into remission. Aside from an occasional flu, Jacob's health was good. His life was filled with school and his love for maple-walnut ice cream, foot-long hotdogs, and rollerblading.

At nine years old, the battle began: coming out of remission, his only hope would be a bone-marrow transplant. After a battery of tests, the doctors discovered Jacob's sister Samantha was an exact match.

The whole community rallied around Jacob's family. Pizza sales, auctions, and raffles raised money for the family to travel to the hospital.

Clare and Noah, Jacob's mom and dad, were always at their son's side. When the time was right and Jacob was ready, they burned out his bone marrow and transplanted Samantha's marrow into her brother.

A few days before Jacob was ready to be released, a sore appeared on his mouth, which turned out to be the start of an infection. Jacob's health declined. Fevers weakened and exhausted him.

Clare and Noah stayed at their son's bedside. One night Clare was sleeping in the chair and Noah was sitting by Jacob's bed. Jacob opened his eyes, stretched out his small fevered hand, and said:

Hold my hand, Daddy.

I'm afraid.

I hurt so bad.

Noah took his son's hand. Jacob smiled, closed his eyes, and never opened them again. Noah, who has deep faith, closed his eyes and prayed:

Hold my hand, Jesus.

I'm afraid.

I'm hurting.

Who doesn't know the litany of human pains, sufferings, hurts, and troubles that can disappoint and discourage you as they make their way into your life? Norman Vincent Peale once said, "There's only one group of people who don't have problems and they're all dead. Problems are a sign of life. So the more problems you have, the more alive you are."

Handle Your Heartaches

Everything was going great in your relationship, and then it took an unexpected turn. You're alone now. Death or divorce removes your spouse. You ask: "How can I go on?" The routine checkup shows the cough you thought was nothing is cancer. You ask: "Why me?" Married, now divorced. Employed, now fired. Healthy, now terminal. Successful, now barely making it. Life, now death.

Step 7 in the Self-Care Solution is learning to take the time to look at life's heartaches and believe, "Well, it's about time to take them off life-support and claim peace of mind again." You can only have it when you handle your heartaches creatively. How? Jacob and Noah give us a way through a simple prayer:

Hold my hand, Jesus.

I'm afraid.

I'm hurting.

When life hits you with sufferings, sorrows, slaps, setbacks, insults, or injustices you will find relief when you practice "fine-tuning" your thoughts. What works for me is one of my favorite Scripture verses, Philippians 4:8:

> Fix your thoughts on what is true and good and right.
> Think about things that are pure and lovely.
> And dwell on the fine, good things in others.
> Think about all you can praise God for.
> And be glad about it

Saint Paul wrote this verse while in prison, chained to a guard, waiting to be executed. In the midst of heartache, Saint Paul fine-tunes his thoughts, concentrating not on his pain and misery but on positive thoughts, capturing the essence of "positive possibility thinking."

So often when life gets difficult, you can let your thoughts get the best of you. They control you as you replay over and over again what happened to you. You find it hard to shake it loose from your memory and move on. You have a choice. Fine-tune your thoughts to focus on positive possibility thinking, or stay nervous, anxious, worried, and afraid with negative, dead-end thinking, imagining and expecting the worst. Dead-end thinkers' heads are filled with: "I'm beat." "I can't handle this." "It's over." They are overwhelmed, trapped, and powerless.

Positive possibility thinkers' heads are filled with, "Okay, what happened?" "Let me catch my breath, see what happened, and make sense out of this." They open their eyes to see alternatives and opportunities, and look at what they have left. Positive possibility thinkers never quit; knocked down, they pick themselves up and walk again.

As we learn from the adjustments we make in our lives, all your heartaches have the potential to change you. At the bottom of every heartache is "I can't handle whatever life brings me." Illness, mistakes, losing your job, getting old, being alone, losing a loved one, feelings of "I just can't handle it. I'm afraid." The truth is, if you knew you could handle anything that came your way, what would you possibly fear? Nothing. Decrease the fear and increase your ability to handle whatever comes your way through the way you think. Positive possibility thinkers push fear, worry, and anxiety out of their lives and shout: "I can handle this! I'm not giving up!"

Choose correctly. Your choice will determine if you emerge better or bitter, stronger or weaker, encouraged or discouraged, trying or quitting. What matters in life is not what happens to you—what matters is what you do with what happens. When handed lemons, positive possibility thinkers will make lemonade.

Helen Keller, author and speaker, sums up fine-tuning your thoughts through positive possibility thinking when she says, "So much has been given to me. I have no time to dwell on what has been denied."

Heartache-Casting

After you learn to fine-tune your thoughts, complete the process by practicing heartache-casting, using a "turn it over to God" attitude: "Cast your cares upon the Lord who will give you support" (Psalm 55:22), and again, "Cast all your worries upon him because he cares for you" (1 Peter 5:7). Finally, "Come to me, all you who labor and are burdened, and I will give you rest" (Matthew 11:28).

Accept the offer. Brothers and sisters in Jesus's time did. The gospels are packed with stories of lives that were broken and hurting. They believed Jesus would take care of them. The blind, deaf, dying, paralyzed, morally and spiritually bankrupt, and judged cast their heartaches on Jesus. Once they did, their lives were changed for the better.

At every Mass, you can practice heartache-casting by turning your problems over to God. First, listen as the good news of God and Jesus is proclaimed, hearing how they reached out then—and reach out now—in love, warmth, care, and concern to the hurting, lost, forgotten, and unimportant, reminding them they are significant. Then pray as Jesus taught: "Give us today our daily bread," asking Jesus to feed you with what you need at this time, today, in your life to cope and survive. Keep praying these words: "Only say the word and I will be healed." Listen and open your heart to hear the words: Forgive. Accept. Let it go. Try again. Patience. Slow down. Compassion. Stop judging. Love.

Casting your heartaches away and turning them over to God is a trusting process. It's hard, but once you have placed your complete trust in God, you can really say: "Whatever, God. Whatever comes into my life, I believe your love and care will get me through it. I believe God will push, pull, drag, tow, or carry me."

Healing does come, but it takes time. While you are healing, try your best not to be a dead-end thinker. Wallowing in negativity only makes it harder for you to heal. Remember: God can only heal heartaches if you give him all the pieces. Hold nothing back. Leave nothing behind to dwell upon.

When life's heartaches tangle you up, consider this plan as a way to begin casting your heartaches to God:

• *Respect your heartache.* Pay it just the right amount of attention. Take your time. Have no one tell you how you should feel or not feel. It's your heartache.

• *Select your response.* Either negative: dead end, finished, no options. Or positive: endless possibilities, fresh opportunities, and new doors waiting to be opened. Select wisely.

• *Protect yourself from people who carry hurts for years.* People who have been hurt are the ones who hurt people. Watch out for the gloomers and doomers—"It's never gonna get better"—and their relatives, the whiners and complainers—"Oh, it's terrible." Surround yourself with people who say, "I know what you're going through. I've been there. Do you want to pray together?"

• *Reflect on these ageless words*: God grant me serenity to accept the things I cannot change, courage to change the things I can, and wisdom to know the difference. (Reinhold Niebuhr)

Healing from heartaches is difficult, but following these four steps can be easy. Just take it one step at a time, remembering to give your pain over to God every step of the way.

Shake It Off and Step Up

Once upon a time, there was a farmer who had an old mule. The mule fell into a deep, dry well and began to cry loudly. Hearing his mule cry, the farmer came over and assessed the situation. The well was deep and the mule was heavy. He knew it would be difficult, if not impossible, to lift the animal out. Because the mule was old and the well was dry, the farmer decided to bury the animal in the well. In this way he could solve two problems:

put the old mule out of his misery and have his well filled. He called upon his neighbors to help him. To work they went.

Shovel full of dirt after shovel full of dirt began to fall on the mule's back. He became hysterical. Then, all of a sudden, an idea came to the mule. Each time they would throw a shovel full of dirt on his back he could shake it off and step up. Shovel full after shovel full, the mule would shake it off and step up. Now, exhausted and dirty, but quite alive, the mule stepped over the top of the well and walked through the crowd.

Too often, you nurse hurts, keeping them alive inside and going over them time and time again; not only stewing from them, but also chewing them over and over until you get sick. Too often, you rehearse hurts, telling everyone what has happened to you. People will eventually steer clear of you because they are tired of hearing you go on and on about the negative things in your life. You aren't the only one who has been hurt in life. Keep whining about it and you will see others do their best to avoid you. As you rehearse your list of woes, they say to themselves, "get over it already."

You continue to hold on to your problem for weeks, months, even years. You cannot jiggle it loose from your memory; it eats away at you and steals your joy, happiness, and peace of mind. The past hurt can create feelings of bitterness, resentment, anger, and revenge. It never helps to hang on to these painful memories or let them be ghosts in your life, every now and then haunting you. You keep allowing these emotions to be thrown on your back and if you do nothing, you will be buried deep in the well. Walls will be built around you, shutting out people and leaving you to experience nothing but the pains of loneliness.

You have a choice: keep your pain inside and cuddle the hurt, or shake it off and step up. Give it a try. Shake them off and step up: hurtful words or painful actions, shake it off and step up. Let it go. Whatever it is—a rude comment, a past mistake, being ignored—you can stew over it all week. It can occupy you all the time. The cure is to accept what has happened, try to make sense out of it, learn from it, and then shake it off and step up. When you let go, you feel free, because you are no longer buried in the well.

Once you are on your feet again, you can take some action. You can decide where you want to grow in life, the direction you want to take. You can decide whether you will allow the hurt to make you a bitter or a better person. Face your hurts and respond to them positively, refusing to give in to panic, bitterness, or self-pity.

The heartaches and hurts that come along to bury you usually have within them the potential to benefit you. Well, it's about time to decide: turn them over to God, invite God inside your life. Once you have given God your pain, you can shake it off and step up, turning your heartaches into learning experiences, emerging stronger and wiser.

Lighten Up

An Illinois man left the snow-filled streets of Chicago for a vacation in Florida. His wife was on a business trip and was planning to meet him the next day. When he reached his hotel, he decided to send his wife a quick e-mail. Unable to find the scrap of paper on which he had written her e-mail address, he did his best to type it in from memory. Unfortunately, he missed one letter and his note was directed instead to an elderly preacher's wife whose husband had died only the day before.

When the grieving widow checked her e-mail she took one look at the monitor and let out a piercing scream, falling to the floor in a dead faint. At the sound, her family rushed into the room and saw this note on the screen: "Dearest wife: Got checked in. Everything prepared for your arrival tomorrow. P.S. Sure is hot."

Ah! Laughter. I hope this story put a smile in your life. Remember: "Laugh and the world laughs with you. Cry and you simply get wet."

When was the last time you remember walking around with a smile on your face, a laugh in your belly, lightness in your heart, and a sense of joy at the sheer wonder of being alive? Has it been too long?

It's possible to have the twinkle in your eye that comes from inner joy. How? Lighten up. Proverbs sums it all up: "A happy heart is like good medicine, but a broken spirit drains your strength"(15:13).

These days, everyone is too serious. Just look around—people seem to be frustrated and uptight about everything. Some go through life with their fingers on the panic button, one problem after another, trying to control things and make life a certain way. It never works. Life just is as it is. Once we accept this, we become free. To hold on is to always be serious and uptight.

Keep this in mind: positive people laugh to forget hurts, disasters, and pains. Negative people forget to laugh. Laughter is a gift for coping and survival. If lightness is missing from your life, put it back! Lighten up and take a laugh break. Laughter is contagious. Laughter is inner jogging. Laughter reduces pain.

Read Norman Cousins's book, *Anatomy of Illness*, in which he prescribes laughter in large doses to those who are terminally ill. He instructs his patients to watch the classics—*Abbott and Costello, The Honeymooners*, and *I Love Lucy*. Tumors may not shrink or cancer disappear, but laughter gives relief from pain. A wonderful healing power is released each time you laugh. And when one positive emotion is created, it's possible to experience other positive moods.

Well, it's about time to give yourself a well-deserved laugh break! You owe it to yourself. Comics, joke books, and classic comedies are ideal pain relievers with no side effects. When you laugh, all kinds of wonderful things happen to benefit your entire self. You cannot get ulcers when you laugh; you have to choose one or the other. Laughter reminds you that even if you are sad, you are more than your sadness. It can give you the right attitude and power to handle life. It's up to you.

You decide to go through life with gloom and doom, moan and groan, whine and bellyache—or lighten up and laugh. Do you zap the joy, excitement, and preciousness out of life by always dwelling on the bad, the awful, and the terrible? Make the choice! Begin with a smile; it puts you closer to laughing. G.K. Chesterton says it best, "Angels fly because they take themselves lightly."

Better Blocker

Do you ever think of heartaches and hassles as being knots in a ball of string, problems that can be untangled with the right amount of skill and patience? Or do you consider heartache as being as shipwrecked: you feel alone, high and dry, lost, and all by yourself. Shipwrecked. The wind has been taken out of your sails and you wonder, "Will I make it? How can I ever get back on my feet again?" Where do you go to unravel this mess you're in? Isaiah tells us: "Turn to me (God) and be safe" (Isaiah 45:22). These words bring security and comfort, assuring us "everything will be okay."

Pray these words, slowly, silently, and listen: God is here. God is in control. God will find me. Block out the clutter of discouragement, depression, and disappointment, and let these words sink into your heart, as you change your attitude from "nobody cares," to "God cares." Then open your eyes to see the people God has placed into your life to help you find your way again.

Pray two more words: Whatever, God. Whatever life throws at me, I'm ready, because God will not let me be defeated. God's there to help me to untangle the knots as I faithfully pray: "Whatever, God."

Overcoming Adversity

*Birds sing after a storm; why shouldn't people feel as free
to delight in whatever remains to them?*
Rose F. Kennedy

I hear it so often from people:
"Why, God?"
"When is enough going to be enough?"
"How much more do I have to take?"
"Why do bad things happen to good people?"
I wish I knew the answer. Maybe the right question is, "What happens to good people when bad things hit them?" Saint Augustine captures it all when he writes: "God had one son on earth without sin, but never one without suffering."

Alice complained to her father about how hard things were in her life. She did not know how she was going to make it and wanted to give up. She was tired of fighting and struggling. It seemed as one problem was solved, a new one arose.

Alice's father's solution can help us. Her father, a chef, took her to the kitchen. He filled three pots with water and placed each on a high fire. Soon the pots came to a boil. In one he placed carrots, in the second he placed eggs, and in the last he placed ground coffee beans. He let them sit and boil. He told his daughter that water was adversity that brings hardships, sufferings, misfortunes, hurts, and all kinds of nasty things into people's lives.

Alice waited impatiently, wondering what her father was doing. In about twenty minutes, he turned off the burners. He

71

fished the carrots out and placed them in a bowl.

"Watch and learn, Alice. Always pay attention to your reaction to life's adversities. When you pay attention you will survive and not be destroyed. Look at the carrots. Before they hit the boiling water, they were strong, hard, and firm. Once they gave in to the boiling water and didn't control their reaction to it, they wilted and lost their strength. At one time they were strong, but now weak and soft to the point of falling apart."

He pulled the eggs out and placed them in a bowl. "Watch and learn. The egg is fragile. The outer shell protects its liquid interior. After a few minutes in the boiling water the eggs are changed." Alice's dad cracked open the egg and showed her that while the shell was the same, the inside was different, no longer soft but hard.

He then said, "Alice, adversity has the same effect on us. Before the storms of life hit us we are soft and gentle, but the death, divorce, and breakups make us hard."

Then Alice's dad scooped the coffee out and placed it in a bowl, asking her to sip the coffee. She smiled as she tasted its rich flavor. She humbly asked, "What does it mean, Dad?"

"The coffee beans changed the water. Sure the adversity stings, but when you are in control of your reactions, even when things look bad, you can make them better."

Are we a carrot that seems hard, but with pain and adversity do we wilt and become soft and lose our strength? When we run into despairing problems, obstacles, or difficulties do we lose our strength to fear, worry, anxiety, and anger, ultimately falling apart?

Are we the egg, which starts off with a malleable heart? Are we hurting people who keep it all inside and it turns our hearts to stone? Do we become stiff when we hear news that isn't good about our health? When words are exchanged in an argument and tension develops, do our hearts become tough?

The negative emotions of anger and guilt can make our hearts hard. We need to experience them when they are inside our guts, own them, and then dump them, or these enemies will end up destroying us.

Are we coffee beans? The ground coffee beans were unique: instead of changing in the boiling water, they changed the water itself. The bean changes the hot water, the thing that is bringing the pain, to its peak flavor when it reaches 212 degrees Fahrenheit. When the water gets the hottest, it just tastes better. If we are like the bean, when things are at their worst, we get better and make things better around us. Step 8 in the Self-Care Solution is to learn from adversity, don't collapse and become negative.

Accentuate the Positive

The next time things don't seem to be going the way we want, consider the positive aspects: What's the benefit in the adversity? When adversity knocks on our door, how do we respond? As a carrot, an egg, or a coffee bean? Adversity shows us what we are made of and can bring out the best in our attitudes: learning to thrive in adverse conditions will help you find greater enjoyment in life and learn more in the process.

Adversity is often called an obstacle or a barrier. Yet it is much more. It is alive in our daily experiences. When adversity occurs, it brings with it an array of emotions. When it strikes, it sometimes makes us sad, disappointed, and regretful. When it is there with us, its hidden advantage is also there. Adversity's presence is our opportunity to succeed by moving on with our lives. Any time we don't seize the moment to get back on our feet, adversity remains, often in the form of pain or regret. When we are courageous enough to seize the opportunity to focus on the positive, we will become victorious in the presence of adversity. Take some quiet time to look through your life and recall the adversities you encountered. Begin to see them for what they are—stepping stones to a better life!

An old Jewish legend tells about a king who asked a jeweler to design a ring, inscribing words on the band that would be appropriate at difficult times. A month later, the jeweler brought the king a ring inscribed with, "This too shall pass." On difficult days the king would read the inscription and be reassured.

Adversity will not last forever. Everything in life comes to a point of completion, as do all the sufferings and difficulties we experience. What will linger is our ability to survive, as we look deep into the eye of the storm knocking us around.

While no single skill or attribute distinguishes resilient people from others, they share similar characteristics, such as confidence in their own abilities and feelings of power rather than powerlessness when making changes, because they're in the driver's seat of their life, and asking for help when it is needed.

There's no sure-fire formula for bouncing back from adversity. Your ability to cope is affected by your personality, support system, and, of course, the severity of the setback. Let me suggest three steps on how to bounce back. They're as easy as ABC.

• *Always find someone to talk with.* Don't try it to go through it by yourself, straining and complaining. It's a long road when you try to face rough times alone. Talking to another person can give you a different perspective or suggest options you haven't even considered. All people experience adversities similar to your own.

• *Believe everything will turn out right.* Say aloud every day, "Let my heart not be troubled, nor be afraid" (John 14:1). Hold on, there will be a tomorrow. As you struggle with the pain, you wonder if it will ever end. It does—bad times are temporary and surmountable.

• *Cast all worry aside.* It's time to stop stewing and start doing. Adversity introduces you to yourself. Focus on what needs to be changed in you and in your attitudes, and get to work doing it. Oprah Winfrey is correct: "Turn your wounds into wisdom." This can become an opportune time to reexamine goals and gain some insight into you and your relationships.

I talked to a mother who experienced one adversity after another. Her husband died in his sleep, leaving her with a string of gambling debts. Her only son was serving a twenty-five-year prison sentence for armed robbery. She told me her life had been miserable. But beneath it all, she knew Jesus was going to get her through and everything would be okay. She prayed and worked every day, learning to sweep up the pieces of her life and go on.

Here is a great therapy for overcoming adversity: it's called resilience, the ability to bounce back from adversity with strength, through a positive attitude. A metaphor from nature can help here. Consider the green twig with its vital, living core; when you step on it or bend it, it springs back. Resilient people have a similar inner life force that allows them to spring back from adversity and pick up the pieces and carry on.

As you read these words, your heart may be wounded. We all have our own stories to tell of failures, tragedies, betrayals, and sometimes just silent years of hurt. We may even have felt like saying, "See you, world, I'm out of here." Adversity has within it the potential to bruise us, leaving us filled with self-pity and panic. But it also has within it the potential to bless us, opening our eyes to see life and people differently.

Every setback and failure we experience also comes with a great possibility. When one door closes, a window of choices opens. The key is to look for the possibility and avoid dwelling on failure. Therefore we will learn things in adversity that we would never have discovered without trouble and we're happy to close out that chapter in our lives and begin again.

Practice this simple remedy: sweep up the pieces and go on. Elton John's words are appropriate:

I'm still standing better than I ever have
Been looking like a survivor.
I'm still standing all this time.
Picking up the pieces of my life
Without all this on my mind.
I'm still standing.

How about you? Are you standing up or lying flat on your back? Are you sweeping up the pieces and going on or wondering where you go from here?

Whatever it is—a disrespectful comment, a past slip-up, an unworkable relationship—stop letting adversity haunt your life. We have the power to exorcise it from our minds.

Sometimes struggles are exactly what we need in our life. If nature allowed us to go through our life without any obstacles, it would cripple us. We would not be as strong as what we could have been.

This story illustrates that point. A man found a cocoon of a butterfly. One day a small opening appeared, and he sat and watched the butterfly for several hours as it struggled to force its body through that little hole. Then it seemed to stop making any progress, appearing as if it had gotten as far as it could and could go no farther.

Then the man decided to help the butterfly, so he took a pair of scissors and snipped off the remaining bit of the cocoon. The butterfly emerged easily, but it had a swollen body and small, shriveled wings. The man continued to watch the butterfly, because he expected that, at any moment, the wings would enlarge and expand to be able to support the body, which would contract in time.

Neither happened! In fact, the butterfly spent the rest of its life crawling around with a swollen body and shriveled wings. It was never able to fly. What the man in his kindness and haste did not understand was that the restricting cocoon and the struggle required for the butterfly to get through the tiny opening were God's way of forcing fluid from the body of the butterfly into its wings so that it would be ready for flight once it achieved its freedom from the cocoon.

It's All About Attitude

A positive attitude or outlook on life can lead to positive behavior and bring peace into our lives. An upbeat, positive person draws other people like a magnet. After all, who would we rather be around—someone who is strong and motivated, with the confidence to keep moving forward, or someone who stays stuck in one place, thinking of reasons why things don't seem to happen?

Negativity is a cancer that only begets more negativity. We all know a Negative Nancy or Negative Nicholas. Life has just been terrible to them. They couldn't say something positive if their lives depended on it. This couple has an Academy Award for the best whining, complaining, bellyaching, and blaming in the neighborhood, but every year they are up for another nomination. They are so negative that they can even ruin a perfectly bad day!

When they die, nothing will change. Here's the scenario. They arrive at the pearly gates. Jesus is talking with Saint Peter and he asks, "Who will be arriving today?" Peter has a grin on his face and says, "Negative Nancy and Negative Nicholas, and today is my day to go fishing."

So Jesus stands and the couple arrives. Immediately, Nancy starts

complaining, "These wings are so heavy and this gown isn't my size."
Nicholas chimes in, "What's my sister doing here? She got Ma's
house, which I should have gotten."

Jesus waits patiently as they unload years of negativity. Then
Negative Nancy asks, "Is that Pavarotti singing the "Ave Maria"?

Jesus says, "Yes, do you like it?"

"Absolutely not, I want to hear Perry Como singing it."

Then Jesus says three words, and when he says them they're for real.
We all know those three words: go to hell. There, the devil has thought
of everything. Hell is a movie theater with a gigantic screen playing
Negative Nancy and Nicholas's life over and over. The popcorn has no
salt and butter. The coffee is cold and the soda warm. It's what negative people deserve. Their attitude has dampened and hurt other people's lives.

So when you see negative people coming, go the other way. Turn on
your negative detector: "Warning, warning, Negative Nancy is
approaching—run and hide." It's simple to understand what life returns
to us when we are negative: less than we started with—nothing.

Our general outlook on life and approach to the world around us
affects everything we do in life. It is about choice in emotional
response. People with this ability choose their own focus, regardless of
the circumstance. They tend to remain in a resourceful state, making
the most of whatever life offers them. Having choice in their attitudes
and focus allows them to live the present moment, create good memories, and project a positive presence to all around them.

Have you ever felt you could do no wrong and that you were on a
roll? It seemed like everything in your life was falling into place, even
if just for a short while. I bet we remember other times too, when
nothing seemed to go right, when we seemed to be running into one
wall after another, always playing catch-up. So what's the difference?
It's still you! All that's changed is our own attitude.

Attitudes can even be detected in the words we use. For example, "I
will" indicates choice, whereas "I can't" indicates powerlessness. Our
attitude is not determined by circumstances, but by how we respond
to those circumstances. Our mind determines our attitude; think,
"beat and finished," and we are. We always have the choice to respond

either positively or negatively. What happens to us is less important than what happens within us. "Our life is what our thoughts make it," noted the Roman philosopher Marcus Aurelius.

One day in a doctor's waiting room, my friend Judy noticed a young boy playing with toy soldiers. Judy noticed that the boy wore a patch over one eye, and she marveled at how unaffected he seemed to be by his loss. Engaging the boy in conversation, she eventually asked what had happened to his eye. He considered her question carefully, and then replied simply, "There's nothing wrong with my eye. I'm a pirate!" and then he went back to playing with his soldiers.

Attitude is our chief weapon we use to fight in all the wars and battles we encounter throughout our lives. Clarence Blasier says, "The obstacles you face are...mental barriers, which can be broken by adopting a more positive approach." People with a positive attitude are not living in denial of adversity, troubles, or difficulties, but have a healthy and mature grip on life. We can either crawl under the covers and never come out to live, or take each day as it comes, avoiding the temptation to overreact and spiral out of control. We need to believe that only we can control our attitude in any situation. Remember this wonderful ten-word philosophy: "If it is to be, it is up to me." That's a positive attitude.

Gratitude Moments

Often when we think we have it all together, something will happen in our lives to remind us we'll never have it together. The older we get, the more we realize that when we get one wall up, the others come tumbling down. We need to accept what life hands us. Proverbs 3:5–6 makes so much sense: "Trust in the Lord with all your heart, and lean not on your own understanding; in all your ways acknowledge him and he shall direct your paths." The adversities will always be there, but God will always be there, too, and that gives us the edge.

It's what writer Bette Howland tells us: "For a long time it seemed to me that real life was about to begin, but there was always some obstacle in the way. Something had to be got through first, some unfinished business; time still to be served, a debt to be paid. Then life would begin. At last it dawned on me that these obstacles were my life."

Well, it's about time we changed our negative thoughts into positive ones. We can't change and control the world, but we can change and control our attitude as we experience different pressures, circumstances, or adversities. We begin by burying three words: if, can't, and impossible. These words block progress and paralyze motivation. They keep us from seeing that even though life brings adversity, it is still filled with possibilities.

Follow the burial by appointing yourself the CEO of your new company, "Why Not, Inc." Why Not keeps the doors of options opened wide. In the middle of difficulty lies opportunity. Why not stop being overwhelmed and closed-minded, and look for a different way to sweep up the pieces of adversity so we can get on with our lives?

Begin a Gratitude Moment Journal. Each night, before you go to sleep, write down three things you are grateful for. This raises our awareness of the positive aspects of our lives as we recall all the people and things that we have taken for granted when we are caught out in our own little worlds. Daily Gratitude Moments can empower us to change our negative thought patterns into positive ones.

Gratitude Moments fill our hearts with joy, kindness, and happiness, which cannot exist in the same space as self-pity, envy, or bitterness—there's no room for them. Sure, our hearts have been busted up, our minds run through the wringer, but our attitude can still be one of gratitude, focusing on what we still have and not what is missing.

Begin by taking a look within. Open your eyes and recognize that you are an unrepeatable masterpiece of God. Be grateful you have a mind that is curious, creative, and competent, one that possesses rich memories of pleasures and accomplishments. Look within for a sense of humor that brings healing and hope. Become aware of the presence of Jesus, who keeps his promise to live inside our hearts and invites us every day to come a little closer to God.

Then look around. I am grateful for the United States of America and for the thousands of men and women throughout our history who have given their lives for my freedom and yours. I am grateful for the Catholic Church, which allows us to deepen our experience of God and Jesus through word and sacrament. Yes, I am grateful for all those people who have prayed me through adversity and wouldn't leave me until I was able to bounce back and get on with my life.

Look around for the closeness of family who care about you. Remember, it's all about being connected and attached to people who care. A disconnected life is painful, while a connected life will lift us up and tell us we count and matter. C.S. Lewis said, "Christians do not have to consult their checkbook to see how wealthy they are. Just look around and see who is in your life." It's always about people. People who want to hold our hands, stick with us, and get us through it all.

Don't Worry About Tomorrow

Why Not, Inc. must always be prepared for a hostile takeover from Worry. This negative emotion will try to control our attitudes and our lives, taking us places we don't want to go. When we see a potential problem developing, we might spend a lot of time thinking about it: what will happen? what could we do about it? how might we cope?

In scientific terms, worry is described as "a predominantly verbal thought activity concerned with negative views of future events." I like to think of worry as wasting today's time to clutter up tomorrow's opportunities with yesterday's troubles.

Much of our worry is focused on everyday events—making ends meet, dealing with difficult people at work, or trying to decide what to buy or where to send the kids to school. Another type of worry concerns the sorts of things that might happen in the future, such as sickness, accidents, or any other event that might affect our safety or well-being, or that of our families or others we care about.

Most people worry; develop the ability to recognize when worry becomes a problem. It is generally true that all people tend to worry about the same sorts of things, so it is not the content of the worry that is the problem. Instead, worry becomes a problem when it is excessive, difficult to control, too intense, too frequent, or takes up more time than is warranted by the realistic importance of the event or the actual likelihood of the event occurring. Be more realistic. Many people are worried and anxious about events that will never actually happen to them.

Flip through the Bible; it's packed with stories of faith journeys faced with adversity and upsetting situations that could have easily filled people's lives with worry:

Abraham was told to go out and end up where? He didn't know. He could have worried about it, but he believed God would get him safely to his destination, wherever that might be.

Esther could have worried about whether she would be executed for going in to see the king. If she collapsed with excessive worry, would she have gone?

Joseph in prison could have worried that God had forgotten him and that the dreams he had would never come true.

Deborah, when arguing with Barak about the outcome of a campaign, could have worried about whether or not her efforts to get this man to work with her would really produce the proper result.

If these people had been controlled by worry, would they have been effective? That may be why Jesus devoted a large section of the Sermon on the Mount to the topic of worry. He instructs us simply and directly: "Don't worry about everyday life—whether you have enough food, drink, and clothes, your heavenly Father will give you all you need from day to day" (Matthew 6:25).

When struggling with worry, it's good to repeat Jesus's words; "Don't worry about tomorrow." Stop crucifying yourself between the two thieves of regret for yesterday and worry about what tomorrow may bring. Practice living in the present, knowing for certain that yesterday is history and tomorrow may never come. Don't inhibit your potential by brooding over the past and fearing the future. We must do as Jesus instructs; we must focus our energies on the opportunities of today.

HOPE: Hang On. Possibilities Everywhere.
Jesus meant that we should learn to accept situations that we cannot change or those we have limited control over; he didn't mean that we should sit back and do nothing to improve our circumstances. We are to face tough times without worry, while trusting God and taking appropriate steps toward improving the situation. We don't have to be prisoners of worry.

Zip, a carpenter, had just finished a rough day on the job. A flat tire made him lose an hour of work, his electric saw quit working, and now his old pickup truck refused to start. While Fred, his foreman, drove him home, Zip sat in stone silence. Arriving at home, Zip invited his boss to come in and meet his family. As they walked toward the house, the carpenter paused briefly at a large maple tree, touching the tips of the branches with both hands.

When he opened the front door, Zip underwent an amazing transformation. His tanned faced glowed with smiles and hugs for his two small children; then he gave a long embrace and kiss to his wife. After a while, he walked his boss back to the car. They passed the maple tree, and the foreman's curiosity got the best of him. He asked Zip about the "tree ritual" he had seen him do earlier.

"Oh, that's my trouble tree," Zip replied. "I know I can't help having troubles on the job, but one thing is for sure, troubles and frustrations shouldn't be brought home at the end of the day. So, I stop by the maple tree and visualize hanging on it whatever troubles, frustrations, and worries I have."

Then Zip smiled and said, "It's funny, Fred, when I come out in the morning to pick them up again, there aren't nearly as many as I remember hanging up the night before."

In life, we have a choice: we can allow what has happened or what may or may not happen fill our heads and lives with negative, dead-end, hopeless thinking, or we can hang up all those worries and then live by the motto of Why Not, Inc., HOPE, which means Hang On. Possibilities Everywhere, the secret of life for keeping the flames of hope burning and alive. It can only be experienced when we start looking in the right direction and throwing out of our lives everything that brings us down and keeps us from feeling things will work out fine. John Foster Dulles sums it up best when he writes: "The measure of success is not whether you have a tough problem to deal with, but whether it's the same problem you had last year."

Isaiah tells us, "Turn to me (God) and be safe" (45:22). Let our prayer always be, "God, I'm ready for whatever." Bring life on. It can be a battle and how we emerge is up to us. Keep saying the prayer over and over, until you believe it.

Winston Churchill is so accurate when he says: "When I look back on all these worries, I remember the story of the old man who said on his deathbed that he'd had a lot of trouble in his life, most of which never happened." I would add this: "One day you'll look back on all this and laugh."

Better Blocker

A mother was convinced that her son should become a Christian. She pleaded with him to come to the faith and sent him little cards with Bible verses on them, tapes with sermons, and spiritual books, but all to no avail.

One day, she fell to her knees and begged God that He would totally remove the one obstacle to her son's conversion.

There was a blinding flash, and...*pooof*...she disappeared.

This story reminds me of an old Chinese curse: may you get what you wish for. Or as Garth Brooks says, "Some of God's greatest gifts are unanswered prayers."

Take control of your life, get out of your way, and stop letting hardships, misfortunes, and pains completely overwhelm you. Opportunity may knock only once, but adversity leans on the doorbell. Worries always find you, and when they do, how are you going to manage them?

The Self-Care Solution offers an approach when they arrive. It's not letting the adversities depress you, but impress you with choices. Your positive or negative reaction to difficulties determines the amount of happiness you will experience. There comes a time when troubles and difficulties seem to gang up on you.

When the Japanese mend broken objects, they aggrandize the damage by filling the cracks with gold. They believe that when something has suffered damage and has a history, it becomes more beautiful. So will you.

Talking with the Shepherd

*Trust is putting all your eggs in Jesus's basket
and counting your blessings before they hatch.*
Unknown

A grandfather and his granddaughter were in the backyard before supper. The little girl asked him, "Grandpa, you seem to know everything. Could you tell me where Jesus lives?"

Smiling, he picked up his granddaughter and said, "Look into the bottom of this well. What do you see?"

"I can only see myself in the water," said the little girl.

"Great, that's where Jesus lives," responded the grandfather.

Friends of mine have a sign on the wall in their guest bedroom: Don't Count Sheep, Talk to the Shepherd. This is a great insight into what we do when we pray. Prayer is a conversation with Jesus who knows us best and loves us completely. Before turning to prayer, we need to look at the images of Jesus we have held throughout our lives, which can influence our ability to pray and our quality of prayer. If we imagine or see Jesus as demanding and accusing, then we will most likely have a difficult time feeling genuinely close to the shepherd. If we envision Jesus as cruel and uncaring, then we will certainly have a difficult time connecting to Jesus in prayer, Step 9 of the Self-Care Solution.

Who is the Jesus that lives deep inside us? Who is the Jesus who has made his home inside our lives? We carry inside ourselves images of Jesus; most, if not all, come from our childhood and what people who are significant to us have taught us about Jesus.

Is it hard for you to have an image of Jesus that might be different from the one that the church, your parents, or others have presented to you in the past? Take this time to find out who Jesus truly is in your personal life. At some point along the spiritual journey, as you make your way through the Self-Care Solution, you need to understand Jesus and the distorted images you have used in the past to try to connect to Jesus.

Most, if not all, of the images we carry inside are false and can keep Jesus at a distance. Well, it's about time we look again at all the false images we have adopted concerning Jesus, and get rid of them so we welcome healthy images of Jesus. Once we do, we can deepen our prayer relationship.

One image is of the Jesus who is out to get us. We call this "Jesus, the Gotcha God." He's sneaky. He hides behind corners. The minute we do something wrong, He jumps out in front of us and shouts, "Gotcha!" He's only out to catch us doing something wrong. He's not on our side.

Then we have "Jesus, the Santa Claus God." This image conjures up a wise, generous, and jolly old man who sits on his throne in heaven, making a list of what we do or don't do—and then he checks it twice. He knows when we have been bad or good. Every move we make, he knows. He's out to label us a loser and keeps a record of all of our mistakes and failures. Then when we die and stand before him, he reads it all back to us and passes a judgment, because the Santa Claus God doesn't forget anything.

We also have the "let's-make-a-deal-with-Jesus God." We have all worshipped at Jesus's feet. When life deals us a setback or unfairness, or when we are looking for positive results, we bargain with Jesus. There's the "if" condition, followed by our guarantee of what we will do. The "if" part of the deal is what we expect from Jesus, anything from good news from our doctors, to a college acceptance, to getting the job we wanted. The "what we will do" part of the deal is our promise to pay Jesus back in return for the favor he gives to us. It can be a sacrifice we will make, changing a bad habit, or doing something for somebody else. For example, "If the tests come back favorable from radiology, then I will give up sweets for two months." Playing the "let's make a deal" game with Jesus can result in our being angry with him when the outcome isn't what we expected. It's expressed by asking,

"Why are you doing this to me?" "Didn't I prove I loved you?" Stop getting into the practice of making deals with Jesus. It leaves us with bad feelings when things just don't turn out like we bargained they would.

Don't forget about the "Intimidator Jesus." In this model, Jesus uses fear to keep us in our place. Growing up, most of us were afraid of Jesus. We were told that Jesus would punish us for lying. Our parents or Sunday School teachers said, "Jesus is so disappointed in you when you act that way," or, "Go to your room and ask Jesus to forgive you for your bad attitude." We would never dare to step out of line, because the intimidator will become the "Terminator Jesus" and wipe us out forever.

Finally, we have the "Jesus Who Wills It." This is how we try and save Jesus's reputation. We use it to soothe the blow when tragedy happens. We respond by saying, "Well, it's Jesus's will." Is it? I struggle with this, as do others, especially when it has to do with children dying before their parents or a disaster that takes the lives of many people. I have heard people say, "Now I know for sure Jesus loves me. Jesus made me miss the plane and I didn't get killed." How about those people who made the flight—did Jesus love them? I think so. We have to be careful when we try to give simple answers to life's pains and sufferings by rationalizing everything with Jesus's will.

We cannot connect and relate with Jesus in a healthy relationship built on any of these twisted images. They hold us back and keep us from getting close to Jesus and sharing with him all that's going on in our lives. As adults, we need to disconnect with those distorted images and reconnect with the reality of who Jesus is and all Jesus can be in our lives.

Reconnect with Jesus

Spiritual writer Edward Farrell tells this beautiful story. A priest and an elderly gentleman were walking one day along the streets. As they walked, they talked along the way. Suddenly, a storm began to develop, so they took shelter and waited for a bus. After their conversation moved to silence, the elderly gentleman took out a prayer book and began to pray half aloud. The priest noticed a peace and holiness surrounding the man. So without thinking the priest said, "You must think Jesus loves you." The man closed his prayer book, looked up at the priest, and smiled deeply, saying, "Yes, Jesus is very fond of me."

This is our starting point. Take a deep breath, smile deeply, and hear Jesus whisper, "I take pleasure in you, my child." We need to reconnect with a healthy image of the Jesus who lives inside each one of us.

Jesus delights in us. We are not made by chance or accident but created with a purpose. After God fashions us into his image and likeness, he steps back, probably saying, "ahhh," and speaks the affirmation to accentuate and to attach importance to the quality of his work: "Very good." Jesus delights in every person God has created. With gentleness and patience, he related to them because he had the eyes to see beyond the outside to the inside. He knew what Samuel wrote, "We judge the outside appearance while God looks inside first" (16:7). When we hear this, we should be encouraged and not discouraged, because Jesus revels, appreciates, enjoys, savors, values, cherishes, and treasures us.

And Jesus was aware of two wonderful passages from Isaiah, referring to them throughout his ministry. First he writes, "Can a mother forget her infant, be without tenderness for the child of her womb? Even should she forget, I will never forget you. See, upon the palms of my hands I have written your name" (49:15–16). And then he tells us, "But now, says the Lord, who created you, O Jacob, and formed you, O Israel: Fear not, for I have redeemed you; I have called you by name; and you are mine."

Jesus invites us to experience a tender, loving God. Jesus's nature is love, and he loves unconditionally, completely, and absolutely. We cannot win this love, lose it, or earn it, but we can refuse it. This is our choice. Jesus loves us with no strings attached and is not concerned about our "priors"—our "wasness" doesn't matter to him. It's who we are in the process of becoming at this moment that counts. We can't change our yesterdays. We can only grow and know we have power through our connection with Jesus to make today a different day. This is a healthy image to carry inside as we bond with Jesus.

Jesus did not appear on the earth, and then disappear from our lives. He's not waiting until we trip and fall. He's intimately involved with us, urging and supporting us with every step we take. He delights in us and invites us to take part in his word. Because he does, we want to do the right thing and act responsibly toward another. Just knowing we are loved gives us the strength to live a good life.

Join these positive visions of Jesus with another image we need to carry inside. There's a wonderful quote by the famous author, Unknown, that says, "Jesus loves me just as I am, but Jesus loves me too much to let me stay the way I am." Jesus stirs up a desire inside of us to always grow and become more of whom we are capable of being.

This is what Jesus does. He fans the flames to get God's people infected with enthusiasm. From time to time, we need to allow Jesus to inject us with a fresh shot of enthusiasm in many areas of our lives. Sometimes, we just need to do something different to get out of a rut. Other times, we need to change our attitude, or overcome feelings of depression, frustration, anger, or hopelessness.

Jesus is God's own definition of himself. We would be hard pressed to find any of those distorted images of Jesus in his ministry. Jesus smashed those twisted images. People experienced in Jesus know he is a God who has always been on their side and who wants to become friends. Jesus used kindness, understanding, compassion, care, concern, love, and forgiveness as opposed to fear, punishment, or retaliation, to motivate people to put aside their old habits and behaviors. These life-nurturing qualities triggered a wholesome image of love, communicating to everyone there is hope, never give up, Jesus is in your corner.

Prayer as a Second Language

The mother mouse knew that sooner or later she'd have to introduce her little mice to the real world, so the day came when she said, "Children, come with me, we're venturing outside."

So they all gathered around Mamma Mouse, poking their heads through the mouse hole and walking outside. Right there, a big black cat was sleeping.

Mamma Mouse's heart was pounding, but she decided these kids had to learn about life sooner or later. She tiptoed with her babies around the sleeping cat, who suddenly opened one eye and raised his paw. Mamma Mouse arched her back and let out two heavy barks and the cat went running out of the room.

She turned to her children and said, "Kids, I want you to know that when you get into a tight spot, it always helps to know a second language."

Prayer is our second language. Once we connect with Jesus, we need to communicate with him to stay spiritually and psychologically alive. Talking with Jesus gives us a look into who we are, what we have, and what we do. When we stop praying, we will slowly fall apart. Prayer helps to keep our lives focus and directed.

The purpose of prayer is to slow us down, so we can see clearly into ourselves and become fully present in each moment as we gain an understanding of the way things are. Through prayer, we invite Jesus inside our lives and circumstances. In order to have inner tranquility, we need to discover what is preventing us from accessing peace—the messes, the clutter, the noise—and block all of it out, keeping Jesus in our lives.

What is missing in your prayer life? Has prayer been challenging for you? Do you feel truly connected to Jesus when you pray? Do you experience being one with Jesus? Have you ever asked Jesus what was in the way when you prayed and have not felt connected? This in itself is an honest and soul-searching prayer.

Being honest and real before Jesus is what prayer is really all about! The best way I know of getting to know someone, or to become intimate in a relationship is to share your heart and soul with that person. Jesus would like nothing more than for you to do this with Him. Jesus is love and therefore is drawing you into a loving and nurturing relationship in order that you may experience blessings each day.

Prayer can be a difficult task. To whom, or to what, do you address your prayer? What do you seek in your prayers? Are you informing Jesus of your needs, hoping they will be satisfied? Are you asking for peace on earth for all people? Do you get on your knees and close your eyes, hold beads, attend church, chant a mantra, say a novena, or recite a list of miseries you need relief from? Is there a formula that guarantees you will be heard? How often do you—should you—pray? These questions speak to our common experience about praying and the nature of prayer.

Emily asked the local pastor, Father Michael, to come to anoint and pray with her father, Andy. When the pastor arrived, he found Andy lying in bed with his head propped up on two pillows and an empty chair beside his bed. The priest assumed that the old man had been informed of his visit. "I guess you were expecting me," the priest said.

"No, who are you?" said the bedridden man. "Oh yeah, the chair. Would you mind closing the door?" Puzzled, the pastor shut the door.

"I've never told anyone this, not even my daughter," said Andy. "But all of my life I have never known how to pray. At church, I used to hear the pastor talk about prayer, but it always went right over my head.

"I abandoned any attempt at prayer," Andy continued, "until one day, about four years ago, when my best friend Dave said to me, 'Andy, prayer is just a simple matter of having a conversation with Jesus. Here's what I suggest. Place an empty chair in front of you, and in faith see Jesus on the chair. It's not spooky because he promised he would be with us always. Then, just speak to him and listen in the same way you're doing with me right now.'

"So, I tried it and I've liked it so much that I do it a couple of hours every day. I'm careful, though. If my daughter saw me talking to an empty chair, she'd either have a nervous break-down or send me off to the funny farm."

Father Michael was deeply moved by the story and encouraged Andy to continue on the journey. Then he anointed him and prayed with him, and returned to the church.

Two nights after Father Michael's visit with Andy, Emily called him to say her daddy had died that afternoon. "Did he seem to die in peace?" Father Michael asked.

"Yes," Emily replied, "When I left the house around two o'clock, he called me over to his bedside, told me one of his corny jokes, and kissed me on the cheek. When I got back from the store an hour later, I found him dead. But there was something strange—in fact, beyond strange. It was kind of weird. Daddy was no longer in bed, but sitting on the floor with his head resting on the seat of the chair."

The wish to pray is a prayer in itself, and Jesus can ask no more of us than that. This idea is closely allied with accounts in the synoptic gospels, which describe Jesus's experience with prayer. For Jesus, prayer is a personal act, committed alone and probably in silence. It's similar to Jesus's teaching on prayer before the Lord's Prayer: "When you pray, go into your room, close your door and pray to your Father who is in secret, and your Father who sees what is done in secret will reward you. When you are praying, do not babble like the pagans, who think that they will be heard because of their many words. Do not act like them. Your Father knows what you need before you ask him" (Matthew 6:6–8).

Mother Teresa cautions in her book, *No Greater Love*, for us to, "Let free our minds. Let's not pray long, drawn-out prayers, but let's pray short ones, full of love."

It's All About Trust

Andy's story puts the power in prayer. When we go through difficult times in life, we ask: "What just happened to me?" It feels like the rug was pulled right out from under us. Life isn't fair. There is a lopsidedness and randomness to life's distribution of windfalls and pitfalls. Who will get sick? Who will be rich? Who will be beautiful?

The psalmist knew the experience and wrote about it with disarming frankness:

> As for me, my foot had almost slipped;
> I had nearly lost my foothold
>   for I envied the arrogant
>   when I saw the prosperity of the wicked.
> They have no struggles;
>   their bodies are healthy and strong.
> They are free from the burdens common to all;
> They are not plagued by human ills...
> Surely in vain I have kept my heart pure;
> In vain have I washed my hands in innocence.
> All day long I have been plagued;
> I have been punished every morning.
>   Psalm 73:2–5, 13–14

Any one of us could have written these words. Life is unfair and that's okay. When it is, pray and tap into the power—trust.

Trust is vital for a wholesome relationship. When we say, "I don't trust you," we keep each other at a distance and play it safe. We share little or nothing about ourselves. The relationship at best is superficial. Walls are built and we say, "That's far enough, don't come any closer."

What a difference when we say, "I trust you." Everything changes. Now we invite others into our lives, telling them, "Come into my life and let me tell you about me." We think, "I feel okay with the other person. I want to get closer and share my thoughts, feelings, hopes, dreams, values, joys, as well as my frustrations, weaknesses, and hurts. I believe the other person will understand, not judge, help, not hurt, and heal, not make it worse. I share everything, holding nothing back."

Trust doesn't happen all at once. We grow in trust, and the deeper we grow, the more we reveal about ourselves, becoming vulnerable and real. We know it's a comfort to have one person we can run to when things fall apart—we trust their love will help them accept us and give us the room to cry, yell, and scream. We feel safe with them. They let us get it all out and stick by us as we put our lives back together and go on living.

We can have the same relationship with Jesus as Andy learned: "It's easy—just speak to him and listen." It begins with two simple words: I surrender. Surrender means you give up thinking you have to go through life alone. The most practical way to live life is to depend on Jesus. In prayer, we recognize not only our need, but also that Jesus is the one who will meet our need. We come before Jesus with empty hands, having nothing to offer but our need.

We have all heard a child say, "I can do it myself." The parent watches as the child attempts to do so. The child may make a mess of things, until in frustration the child cries out for help. How often is this the situation in our own lives? When we first try to do things ourselves, and they end up in chaos, then we get upset and say, "I surrender. Help me."

Saying you surrender, that you want and need help, is your invitation to ask Jesus to come into your life, stay with you, and help you. Often we play games with Jesus. We surrender parts of our lives. We feel that maybe if Jesus knew us completely, he wouldn't like us. So we hide the bad parts from him. We surrender our problems to Jesus for a limited time, or tell him only certain parts.

Consider when Peter saw Jesus walking on the water (Matthew 14:25–36). Peter jumped out of the boat and started walking toward

Jesus. As long as Peter kept his eyes fixed on Jesus and not the waves, he did fine. Once he looked at the waves, he began to sink. There's a lesson for us. We are all surrounded by waves (problems, frustrations, difficulties), but we have a choice. Sink. We let the wave overwhelm, drag us down, and then give up. Swim. We try to handle it by ourselves, foolishly. Surrender. We trust. We reach out and put our hand in Jesus's hand and let him support us and keep us from drowning.

Surrender. Invite Jesus inside your life. Once he's inside, there's no need to be afraid. Jesus will say, "I know everything about you. It doesn't matter. I love you." Talk to Jesus as you talk with a friend. Tell Jesus what's going on in your life. Say, "It's not going good right now, life is a mess," or, "It's getting better," or, "I'm trying to understand what happened." Tell Jesus how you feel: powerless, upset, peaceful, or happy. Leave nothing out.

Invite Jesus In

My grandmother had a picture on her wall of Jesus knocking on a door. I always thought to myself, "What a silly picture. Jesus will never be able to get inside, because the doorknob on the outside is missing." As I grew older, I came to understand what the artist wanted to express through this painting. The door only opens from the inside. It's up to us to invite Jesus in.

I also realized Jesus is a God of persistence. He's going to keep knocking on the door until we open it and say, "Come in." We say to ourselves, "Shhhh. If I don't move and stay quiet, he'll go away." Jesus won't. He just keeps knocking on the door saying, "I know you're in there, let me in." We may crawl in the corner and try to keep him out, but eventually we need to stand up, get on our feet, and rise out of our world of fear; letting Jesus see us in our need so he can help us.

Many years ago, I heard a poem I use when I pray, a simple poem that captures trust. Here it is:

Hold no problem back,
Nothing large, nothing small
When Jesus says, "surrender,"
He wants it all.

Jesus will ask what he asked so many times in the gospels: "What do you want me to do for you?" Your relationship with Jesus will deepen when you say: "Jesus, I need you." Speak from your heart. Say, "Jesus, I need you for direction and guidance: Where is this going to end up? Help me make the right decision. Jesus, I need you for courage and strength. I want to survive. Help me make it. Jesus, I need you for perseverance and determination. Help me to keep on going."

Be quiet. Listen. It's Jesus's turn to talk. Jesus answers all prayers (John 16:23: "Whatever you ask for in my name you will receive.") The answer may not be what we expect, so we feel Jesus hasn't listened. He has. The answer may be "No." Or, "You are not ready." Remember, you're in good company. Moses, King David and even Jesus had their prayer answered with, "No."

I love Celine Dion's song, "Because You Loved Me." In it, she captures for me our prayer relationship with Jesus. I know it isn't a song about praying, but when you read these words, think of Jesus and what Jesus did for you.

You were my strength when I was weak.
You were my voice when I couldn't speak.
You were my eyes when I couldn't see.
You saw the best there was in me.
Lifted me up when I couldn't reach.
I am everything I am because you love me.

Hopefully, these words will ring a bell with you. They are worth repeating, because they give another dimension to our prayer: "I love you and would never leave you. During your times of trial and suffering, when you saw only one set of footprints, it was then that I carried you" (from the poem called "Footprints").

Surrender and allow Jesus to carry you. He will carry you until you are able to get back on your feet and walk again. Trust Jesus enough to invite him into your life, no matter what shape or condition it's in. Talk to him. Tell him what you need and then listen to his gentle voice speak to your heart. Remember Jesus loves you just as you are, but he loves you too much to leave you the way you are. Relief will come. It's an amazing feeling. The heaviness of life is gone.

Everything Depends on God

I love this quote: "Pray as if everything depended on God and work as if everything depended on you." It seems a frog was playing on the rafters of a dairy farm one night and fell into a pail of cream. First he panicked, and then he scrambled for survival, swimming faster and faster. When the farmer came in the next morning, he found the frog standing on a cake of butter, exhausted but happy to be alive.

It's easy to let problems overwhelm us and we stop jumping, hopping, and scrambling for survival. It's easy to give up and stop praying. Often when we feel no immediate answer, it's denial—no, it's a delay. We aren't ready. We need to grow. It means we need to face an unresolved problem or change a bad habit or stop an unhealthy behavior. Once we do our prayer will happen.

Keep praying as if everything depended on God and keep working as if everything depended on you—and watch what happens.

Better Blocker

> One night, a house caught fire and a young boy was forced to run to the roof. The father stood on the ground below with outstretched arms and called to his son, "Jump, I'll catch you."
>
> However, all that the boy could see between himself and his dad were fire and smoke. His father yelled again, "Jump, son! I'll catch you."
>
> But the boy protested, "Daddy, I can't see you."
>
> The father replied, "But I can see you."

This story captures what prayer is about—trust, which is the foundation of your relationship with Jesus.

We trust Jesus for the big things: forgiveness, heaven, and salvation. Sometimes we don't trust Jesus for the little things, hurts, broken relationships, and disappointments. Trust begins when I say to Jesus, "I surrender." Then jump—after all, where else could you fall but into the arms of Jesus? That's all that matters.

Believing the Best
Is Yet to Come

Those who live in the Lord never see each other for the last time.
German Proverb

Harriet was diagnosed with liver cancer. Her doctors told her she only had four months to live. Shocked, angry, and upset, she spent the next few weeks seeing therapists, priests, and ministers to ask what she should do. After Harriet had made the rounds of so many helping professionals, a social worker at the hospital suggested this: "Visit the children's hospital. Talk to children who are dying."

After some reluctance, Harriet decided she would follow the social worker's suggestion. She arrived at the hospital. The elevator doors opened to the children's floor. Children were walking around with baseball caps and scarves covering their heads. Some had no hair. Others were so sick that they were confined to bed. A little girl walked up to Harriet and asked, "Lady, are you going to die?"

Harriet thought to herself, "My God, nobody has ever asked me that question so directly." She responded, "Yes ... yes, I am going to die."

"Are you afraid?" asked the little girl.

"I'm terrified," said Harriet.

"Why, lady? When you die you will see God."

Do you believe those words? "When you die you will see God" is the wisdom of a child that you need to listen to. That's what death is all about: seeing God, being with God, and living forever with God, the final step of the Self-Care Solution.

Yet most of us are afraid of death. We avoid talking about it. We shield children from it. We say, "Let them remember Grandpa and Grandma the way they were when they were alive." We keep children from attending funerals. We tell them, "Grandpa is sleeping." No, he isn't—he's dead. We tell them, "Grandma is gone on a trip." No, she isn't—she's dead.

We are always upset when we hear that death has come to a young person. When people tell others the news that so and so has died, usually the first question is, "Oh, how old were they?" When someone answers, "seventy or eighty," there's a sigh of, "Oh, well she lived a good life." She may have lived a good life, but maybe she wanted to be seventy-one or eighty-one. Why should it be more acceptable for death to come to the old, rather than the young?

The Final Stage of Life

Isn't it strange that we celebrate all stages of growth, yet it is the final stage of growth, death, that we have a difficult time handling? I am not going to pretend death is easy. It isn't. Even when you are prepared for it, it catches you off guard. Death is a thief. When our parents die, our past is stolen from us. A spouse dies, and our present is gone. When a child dies, our future is gone.

Death hurts. It stings. It seems like a bad dream. Death brings an unreality with it; we just can't believe the one we loved is no longer with us as they were just a few moments ago. We go to grab the telephone to call them, or want to stop by for a visit, just to hear their voice or hug them again. We want to plead for just one more day with them. We go to bed and they come to us in our dreams. We feel wonderful. They may speak to us or just be a part of the crowd. I love the words from the song by Celine Dion, "In my dreams I see you, I feel you, that is how I know you go on." Then reality hits us like a sledgehammer: they're dead.

We sometimes respond to death just as Martha did in the gospel.

When Jesus finally came to their home after receiving word that Lazarus had died, notice what Martha says to Jesus: "Lord, if you had been here, my brother would not have died" (John 11:21). In other words, this could have been prevented if Jesus was where he was supposed to be. He arrived later, not when they thought he was going to come to visit them. Martha found her brother's death easier to bear when she could blame Jesus for it.

It's a natural response to Jesus: "Where were you, Lord, when my mother was dying? Where were you, Lord, while my husband suffered slowly and cruelly? Where were you?" It's at these times we need to drop our heads into our hearts and believe that Jesus is closer than we could ever imagine to the person who is suffering. Jesus didn't give Martha a string of platitudes, but affirmed what she believed: death is not the end of the story, but is the beginning of your eternal and everlasting life.

When we are hit with human suffering, we are all bankrupt of words. The ultimate solution to death doesn't rest in cliché, or in saying the right thing, but in God. Jesus responded humanly when he heard the news about his friend, Lazarus: he cried. What people need isn't a sermon, but a hand to hold as they cry and get it all out. I've learned that when grief is the freshest, words should be the fewest. It's important we don't try to give simple answers to a faith-filled, painful reality.

Like the rest of us who have experienced death, we can connect with people because we know what they are going through. I recently sat with one of my former students, James, whose mother at forty-six was on life support due to a blood clot in the brain. He kept trying to hold back the tears, saying, "I have to be strong for my younger brother."

I told him, "No, you don't. It hurts—get it out." He did.

Then James taught me a lesson. He said, "Father, everything is ended in my relationship with my mom. Our last supper together, the last kiss I gave her—it's over." His mother died a few days later.

Death brings all the lasts we experience with the person: the last holiday, vacation, anniversary, birthday, and conversation. Death also brings out memories of all the firsts we experience without them: the first Thanksgiving, Christmas, or Easter. The absence of the person will sting. The atmosphere is cold and empty. There's finality about it. The richness and quality of the person who has died cannot be replaced.

After we get through the ritual of closure—viewing, church service, and burial—reality sets in and the next day doesn't feel any better. Our lives are never the same. They are minus one. People wonder, "How will I be able to go on without my spouse, parent, or child?" or "Does it get any better?" It does, but it takes time. Healing comes slowly. The memories are so full that we brush them away as they invade our minds.

Don't push away your memories of your departed loved ones. Savor them and allow them to be a source of comfort and healing. When your memories run the gamut from wishing you had done this or said this, and beating yourself up for not having said or done that one last thing, don't berate yourself for feeling the way you do. This thinking is normal. Let it all out, but be careful you don't torture yourself by asking, "Should I have done this? Why didn't I notice she was short of breath?"

You will have good days, when you remember the happy memories, and bad days, when you just can't shake the bad ones loose from your mind. There are no rules on how to deal with death or travel through the grieving process, except let it hurt and don't shut down your feelings. Take your time and don't listen to people telling you what you should or should not do. Step back and give yourself the space to cry and scream, if that helps. Hug your loved one's clothes, sit in their chair, or go to their grave and talk to them. Handle things any way you need to. Do whatever has to be done to be healed.

You will experience different stages of emotions and thoughts, from shock when you hear those words, "Your husband is dead," or "I'm sorry, we did all we could, but your mom is gone," to anger felt toward the person dying. I have sat with families when a spouse lets out that anger, "If only he had taken better care of himself," they rage, or, "She never believed in going to doctors."

You might also experience anger with yourself, "Why didn't I do something when Dad had that terrible cough?" You may find yourself negotiating with God. "Just one more hour with my wife," or, "It happened so quickly, I didn't have time to bring the relationship to a close—how about one more day?" You'll feel tremendous sadness, and eventually acceptance, which doesn't mean the person is out of your mind, but that you've accepted their mortal death. The one who has died is inescapably built into your memory, but you are at a point in your grieving you can talk without coming apart. Your eyes still have a glaze over them as you share your experiences, but the pain will begin to decrease.

HUGS

As I've come to experience death and loss over the years, I've developed a plan that has helped a lot. I call this plan HUGS.

Halt. When death comes, everything stops. Life comes to a standstill. Those words, "She is dead," freeze you in your footsteps. You just can't believe what you are hearing. Your routine is on hold for a while. Business doesn't go on as usual. You will feel exhausted; grief has a physical effect on you. You probably will not be eating or sleeping as well as you should. It's all natural; don't think you are weird or different. Everyone experiences "halt" in various degrees.

Unpack. You can't believe this has happened. You are angry with the person for dying and abandoning you. You are sad, lost, confused. You will experience the full range of human emotions when someone dies, and it's important to unpack your feelings so you can understand them. Take them out, be aware of what is going on, and express what is happening. It's valuable to know what is occurring inside of you.

Let those feelings out. It's okay to cry, to be mad—or to smile again. If you have kept it all inside for years, now is the time to release it. Go to the cemetery and talk to your father, mother, husband, wife, or child. Tell them what you are feeling. Get it out. It's not going to go away until you unpack it and deal with it.

Never be too proud to reach out for help. Others know what you are going through—allow them to help you. They are wounded healers on their own journeys; let them guide you and share what will happen. They can tell you tomorrow will not be all that better, and they can also give you some idea of when things will look up.

Give it time. You are hurting and it's painful, like you've been emotionally hit with a tractor-trailer truck. You have an ache in your heart. The death has opened a void in your life. Give it time. You go through your day and after it's over you may not remember what happened or what you did or said. It seems like you're living in a fog, a dream, something unreal. That's acceptable. You are emotionally busted up. When you are injured physically you need to give your body time to heal. The same happens in death. As you unpack your feelings and try to make sense of what happened and how your life will never be the same again, give it time to sink in.

Survive. When death comes knocking at your door, you wonder, "Will I ever be happy again?" or "Will I be able go on without my loved one?" These are questions of survival. The answer? Yes, you will survive. Don't listen to those who say who you have to be at this point at this time. It's your life that has been wounded. You deal with it in your way. As you do, believe you will make it and you will.

Death never leaves you as it found you. It changes you. You will look at life differently. Priorities will seem more important. Death shouts out, "Well, it's about time to look at who matters, what is important, and where I need to focus." It puts everything in perspective so our lives are not cluttered with nonsense.

In the final hours, when those dying are surrounded by their families, they don't say, "Watch the stock market for me or roll over my certificates of deposit." They tend to say things like, "Take care of your mother. Look out for your sister." Death tells us nothing in this world belongs to us: I have never seen an armored car or U-Haul truck in a funeral procession.

Death is very democratic. It doesn't play favorites. It comes to everybody. It doesn't respect fame, age, religion, race, wealth, popularity, or power. It arrives at everyone's doorstep with a message: the time to live is now. The time to love is now. The message of death is life, lived fully, every day, in loving relationships.

It stares you in the face and asks: "Are you living your life, or just existing?" Actor Michael Landon said, "Maybe God should tell us on the day we are born, the day we are going to die, then we wouldn't miss any chance to live life." Maybe God should. Maybe this is what death is reminding us—that we don't have forever. We need to pay attention to life and people now. The tomorrows will eventually run out.

Better Blocker

Every year around Christmas, *It's a Wonderful Life* shows up on the television. Through the character of George Bailey (Jimmy Stewart) we are asked to think about how important it is to live life and appreciate all we have.

Death is always a wake-up call to cherish life now. It's easy to get so stuck living in the past and future that you miss the present, which is filled with potential.

My sister and I went to speak with a gentleman who engraves the date of death on tombstones. Since my sister's husband and our mother died a few months apart, we'd decided it was time to have the work done on the family stone.

Coming back after a few weeks, the dates were carved into the piece of granite, reminding me I have no control of my birth and death dates, but I certainly have control over the dash in between those dates. The dash indicates how wisely I have used my limited, God-given time. It's the small gestures—showing I care about people, the phone call, visit, or card—that can mean a lot. The dash: my life, your life. Are you living it fully, moment by moment, or just existing? It's hard to cram all you missed in life into a few short months of living.

I believe we should add dashes after the date of death. Death is not the end. It's just a pause. In death life is changed as we gain a place with God in heaven forever. This is our final destination.

Life is a gift. Accept it, cut off the ribbon, unwrap it, live it responsibly, and believe the best is yet to come.

Closing Thoughts

J. J. Gambo arrives at the airport and he sees a scale with this sign: Put in twenty-five cents and be amazed at what I can tell you. So he deposits a quarter and the scale says, "Your name is J. J. Gambo, you weigh 185 pounds and you are taking a 2:20 flight to Philadelphia."

He jumps off the scale, scratches his head thinking, "How can the scale know this about me?" Walking a few hundred yards in the airport terminal he finds another scale. He drops in a quarter and the scale says, "Your name is still J. J. Gambo. You still weigh 185 pounds, and you are still taking a 2:20 flight to Philadelphia."

This must be a trick. He goes into the restroom, changes his clothes, and finds a different scale. Putting in another quarter the scale says, "Your name is still J. J. Gambo. You still weigh 185 pounds, but you missed the 2:20 flight to Philadelphia."

The day you arrived into the world God gave you two promises: your life will have meaning and you are going to live forever. Both depend on each other, but remember, what we do here determines the after. You have no one to blame if you miss any opportunity to live the good life.

You have come to the end of the Self-Care Solution. You can:

Stew. Don't take advantage of the opportunities for growth and change the Self-Care Solution has offered. Sit back and do nothing. Just go on existing and living in a rut.

Boo. Laugh and dismiss the Self-Care Solution as impossible or ridiculous. Be cynical and mocking, and put down people who are serious about improving their lives.

Chew. Draw nourishment from the steps outlined in the Self-Care Solution, and find the energy to live your life with meaning and purpose.

Do. Undertake a step a week or a month, integrating each into your life.

I hope that you put the self-care solution into action. I've been a priest for twenty years, and I know people have a tendency to learn something, think about it, and then forget it. Small steps will get you started, enabling you to see unbelievable possibilities opening up for you. Change doesn't happen all at once.

Remember the basics:

- embrace change
- keep it simple
- take care of yourself
- be content to live in the moment
- listen
- manage your thoughts
- laugh
- talk to Jesus
- be quick to love
- forgive
- leave the world a better place when you go to bed at night.

Thomas Edison says, "If we did all the things we are capable of doing, we would literally astound ourselves." Go ahead—don't let anything stand in your way of living your life.

Suggested Resources

Step 1: Embracing Change

Beck, Martha. *Finding Your Own North Star: Claiming the Life You Were Meant to Live*. New York: Crown Publishers, 2001.

Berg, Art. *The Impossible Just Takes A Little Longer: Living with Purpose and Passion*. New York: HarperCollins, 2002.

Berra, Yogi. *When You Come to a Fork in the Road, Take it*. New York: Hyperion, 2001.

Cappannelli, George and Sedena. *Say Yes To Change*. Cincinnati, OH: Walking Stick Press, 2002.

Carlson, Richard. *You Can Be Happy No Matter What: Five Principles for Keeping Life in Perspective*. Novato, CA: New World Library, 1992.

Chaffee, John. *The Thinker's Way: 8 Steps to a Richer Life*. Boston: Little, Brown and Company, 1998.

Cooper, Robert K. *The Other 90%: How to Unlock Your Untapped Potential for Leadership and Life*. New York: Crown Business, 2001.

Covey, Stephen R. *The Seven Habits of Highly Effective People: Restoring the Character Ethic*. New York: Simon and Schuster, 1989.

Edelman, Marian W. *The Measure of Our Success*. Boston: Beacon Press, 1992.

Ells, David. *Creating Your Future. 5 Steps To The Life Of Your Dreams*: Boston: Houghton Mifflin Company, 1998.

Flanagan, C.M. *People and Change*. Hillsdale, NJ: Lawrence Erlbaum Associates, 1990.

Fox, Emmet. *Diagrams for Living*. New York: HarperCollins, 1968.

Glasser, William. *Reality Therapy*. New York: HarperCollins, 1965.

Hallowell, Edward M. *Human Moments: How to Find Meaning and Love in Your Everyday Life*. Deerfield Park, FL: Health Communications, 2001.

Hinckley, Gordon B. *Stand For Something: 10 Neglected Virtues That Will Heal Our Hearts and Homes*. New York: Three Rivers Press, 2000.

His Holiness the Dalai Lama. *The Art of Happiness*. New York: Penguin Books, 1998.

Johnson, Spencer. *The Precious Present*. New York: Doubleday, 1984.

_____. *Who Moved My Cheese?* New York: G.P. Putnam and Sons, 1998.

Kaufman, Barry N. *Happiness is a Choice*. New York: Fawcett Columbine, 1991.

Kushner, Harold. *When All You've Ever Wanted Isn't Enough: The Search For A Life That Matters*. New York: Summit Books, 1986.

Lippe, Toinette. *Nothing Left Over: A Plain and Simple Life*. New York: G.P. Putnam and Sons, 2002.

McGraw, Philip C. *Life Strategies: Doing What Works, Doing What Matters*. New York: Hyperion, 1999.

_____. *The Life Strategies Workbook*. New York: Hyperion, 2000.

Matthews, Andrew. *Being Happy! A Handbook to Greater Confidence and Security*. Los Angeles, CA: Price Stern Sloan, 1998.

Miller, William A. *The Joy of Feeling Good: 8 Keys to a Happy and Abundant Life*. Minneapolis, MN: Augsburg Publishing House, 1986.

Prager, Dennis. *Happiness is a Serious Problem: A Human Nature Repair Manual*. New York: HarperCollins, 1998.

Quindlen, Anna. *A Short Guide to a Happy Life*. New York: Random House, 2000.

Reynolds, Simon. *Become Happy in Eight Minutes*. New York: Plume, 1996.

Richardson, Cheryl. *Stand Up for Your Life*. New York: The Free Press, 2002.

Robinson, Duke. *Too Nice for Your Own Good: How to Stop Making 9 Self-Sabotaging Mistakes*. New York: Warner Books, 1997.

Rogers, Carl. *On Becoming a Person*. Boston: Houghton Mifflin Company, 1961.

Ruiz, Miguel Don. *The Four Agreements*. San Rafael, CA: Amber-Allen Publishing, 1997.

Rusk, Tom and Randy Read. *I Want To Change But I Don't Know How*. Los Angeles, CA: Price Stern Sloan, Inc, 1978.

Schindler, John A. *How To Live 365 Days A Year*. Philadelphia: Running Press, 2002.

Schuller, Robert H. *The Be(Happy) Attitudes: 8 Positive Attitudes That Can Transform Your Life*. New York: Bantam Books, 1985.

Siegel, Bernie. *Love, Medicine, and Miracles*. New York: Harper and Row, 1986.

Seligman. Martin. *Authentic Happiness*. New York: Free Press, 2002.

_____. *What You Can Change and What You Can't: The Ultimate Guide to Self-Improvement*. New York: Alfred A. Knopf, 1994.

Silverman, Robin L. *The Ten Gifts*. New York: St. Martin's Press, 2000.

Smith, Hyrum W. *What Matters Most: The Power of Living Your Values*. New York: Simon and Schuster, 2000.

Taylor, Susan L. *Lessons in Living*. New York: Random House, 2001.

Vanier, Jean. *Becoming Human*. Mahwah, NJ: Paulist Press, 1998.

Step 2: Clearing Out Clutter

Blakeslee, Mermer. *In the YIKES! Zone: A Conversation with Fear*. New York: Dutter, 2002.

Bricker, Woodeen. *365 Saints. Your Daily Guide to the Wisdom and Wonder of their Lives*. San Francisco: HarperCollins, 1995.

Burns, David D. *Feeling Good. The New Mood Therapy*. New York: Avon Books, 1980.

_____. *The Feeling Good Workbook*. New York: Plume, 1989.

Carlson, Richard. *Don't Sweat the Small Stuff...and it's all small stuff*. New York: Hyperion, 1997.

_____. *The Don't Sweat the Small Stuff Workbook*. New York: Hyperion, 1998.

Chodrom, Pema. *The Places That Scare You: A Guide to Fearlessness in Difficult Times*. Boston: Shambhala, 2001.

DeFoore, Bill. *Anger: Deal With It, Stop It From Killing You*. Deerfield Park, FL: Health Communications, 1991.

Ellis, Albert and Irving Becker. *A Guide to Personal Happiness*. Hollywood, CA: Wilshire Book Company, 1982.

Felder, Leonard. *A Fresh Start: How to Let Go of Emotional Baggage and Enjoy Your Life Again*. Scarborough, Ontario: NAL Books, 1987.

Ferder, Fran. *Words Made Flesh: Scripture, Psychology and Human Communication*. Notre Dame, IN: Ave Maria Press, 1986.

Hallowell, Edward M. *Worry: Controlling It and Using It Wisely*. New York: Pantheon Books, 1997.

Harmin, M. *How to Get Rid of Emotions that Give You a Pain in the Neck*. Niles, IL: Argus Communications, 1976.

Hartman, Thomas. *Just a Moment*. Liguori, MO: Triumph Books, 1993.

Helmstetter, Shad. *What to Say When You Talk to Yourself*. New York: Pocket Books, 1986.

Leider, Richard J. and David A. Shapiro. *Repacking Your Bags. Lighten Your Load for the Rest of Your Life*. San Francisco: Berrrett-Koehler Publishers, Inc., 2002.

McKay, Matthew and Patrick Fanning. *Prisoners of Belief: Exposing and Changing Beliefs that Control Your Life*. Oakland, CA: New Harbinger Press, 1991.

Minirth, Frank, Paul Meier and Don Hawkins. *Worry-Free Living*. Nashville, TN: Thomas Nelson Publishers, 1989.

Pearsall, Paul. *The Pleasure Prescription: To Love, to Work, to Play—Life in the Balance*. Alameda, CA: Hunter House Publishers, 1996.

Potter, Beverly. *The Worrywart's Companion*. Berkeley, CA: Wildcat Canyon Press, 1997.

St. James, Elaine. *Simply Your Life*. New York: Hyperion, 1994.

Sills, Judith. *Excess Baggage: Getting Out of Your Own Way*. New York: Viking Press, 1993.

Tavris, Carol. *Anger: The Misunderstood Emotion*. New York: Simon & Schuster, 1982.

Warren, Neil Clark. *Make Anger Your Ally*. Wheaton, IL: Tyndale House Publishers, 1990.

Step 3: Taking Control of Your Life

Augustine. *The Confessions*. Translation by Rex Warner. New York: A Mentor Book, 1963.

Bausch, William J. *The Yellow Brick Road: A Storyteller's Guide to the Spiritual Journey*. Mystic, CT: Twenty-Third Publications, 1999.

Branden, Nathaniel. *How to Raise Your Self-Esteem*. New York: Bantam Books, 1987.

_____. *The Six Pillars of Self-Esteem*. New York: Bantam Books, 1994.

Borysenko, Joan. *Inner Peace for Busy People: 52 Strategies for Transforming Your Life*. Carlsbad, CA: Hay House, Inc., 2001.

Briggs, Dorothy C. *Celebrate Your Self: Enchancing Your Own Self-Esteem*. New York: Doubleday, 1977.

Brockovich, Erin. *Take It from Me: Life's a Struggle, But You Can Win*. New York: McGraw-Hill, 2002.

Brothers, Joyce. *Positive Plus: A Practical Plan for Liking Yourself Better*. New York: G.P. Putnam and Sons, 1994.

Bykofsky, Sheree. *Me Five Years from Now: The Life-Planning Book You Write Yourself*. New York: Warner Books, 1990.

Cleghorn, Patricia. *The Secrets of Self-Esteem: A New Approach for Everyone*. Boston: Element, 1996.

Deep, Sam and Lyle Sussman. *Yes, You Can*. Reading, PA: Addison-Wesley Publishing Company, 1996.

Evans, Patrica. *Controlling People: How to Recognize, Understand, and Deal with People Who Try to Control You*. Avon, MA: Adams Media, 2002.

Frankl, Viktor E. *Man's Search for Meaning*. New York: Pocket Books, 1959.

Freeman, A. and R. DeWolf. *The 10 Dumbest Mistakes Smart People Make and How To Avoid Them: Simple and Sure Techniques for Gaining Greater Control Over Your Life*. New York: HarperCollins, 1992.

Glasser, William. *Choice Theory: A New Psychology of Personal Freedom.* New York: HarperCollins, 1998.

_____. *The Language of Choice Theory.* New York: HarperCollins, 1999.

Hallowell, Edward M. Connect. *12 Vital Ties that Open Your Heart, Lengthen Your Life, and Deepen Your Soul.* New York: Pocket Books, 2000.

Harris, Thomas A. *I'm OK, You're OK.* New York: Avon Books, 1967.

Hay, Louise. *The Power Within You.* Carlsbad, CA: Hay House, Inc, 1991.

Heldman, Mary L. *When Words Hurt: How to Keep Criticism from Undermining Your Self-Esteem.* New York: New Chapter Press, 1988.

Hyde, M. and E. Forsyth. *Know Your Feelings.* New York: Watts, 1975.

Jones, Ann and Susan Schechter. *When Love Goes Wrong: What to Do When You Can't Do Anything Right. Strategies for Women with Controlling Partners.* New York: HarperCollins, 1987.

Keirsey, David and Marilyn Bates. *Please Understand Me: Character and Temperament Types.* Del Mar, CA: Prometheus Nemesis, 1984.

Kinder, Melvyn. *Mastering Your Moods.* New York: Simon and Schuster, 1993.

Kushner, Harold. *Living a Life that Matters: Resolving the Conflict Between Conscience and Success.* New York: Alfred A. Knopf, 2001.

LaRoche, Loretta. *Life Is Not A Stress Rehearsal.* New York: Broadway Books, 2001.

_____. *Relax—You May Only Have A Few Minutes Left.* New York: Broadway Books, 2000.

Lieberman, David. *Get Anyone To Do Anything and Never Feel Powerless Again.* New York: St. Martin's Press, 2000.

Lindenfield, Gael. *Assert Yourself: Discover how to Cope with Criticism, Learn To Say No.* New York: HarperCollins, 1986.

McGraw, Phil. *Self-Matters: Creating Your Life from the Inside Out.* New York: Simon and Schuster, 2001.

_____. *The Self Matters Companion.* New York: The Free Press, 2002.

McKay, Matthew and Patrick Fanning. *Self-Esteem*. Oakland, CA: New Harbinger Publications, 1987.

Palmer, P. *Teen Esteem: A Self-Direction Manual for Young Adults*. Atascadero, CA: Impact Publishers, 1989.

Powell, John. *Why Am I Afraid to Tell You Who I Am?* Niles, IL: Argus Communications, 1969.

Ringer, Robert. *Getting What You Want: The 7 Principles of Rational Living*. New York: G.P. Putnam and Sons, 2000.

Schuller, Robert H. *If It's Going to Be It's Up to Me*. San Francisco: HarperCollins, 1997.

_____. *Self-Esteem: The New Reformation*. Waco, TX: Word Books, 1982.

Sher, Barbara. *Wishcraft: How to Get What You Really Want*. New York: Ballantine Books, 1983.

Sinetar, Marsha. *Do What You Love, the Money Will Follow: Discovering Your Right Livelihood*. New York: Dell, 1987.

Trent, John. *LifeMapping: A Revolutionary Process for Overcoming Your Past, Taking Control of Your Present, and Charting Your Future*. Colorado Springs, CO: Focus on the Family Publishing, 1994.

Vaughan, Susan. *Half Empty, Half Full: How to Take Control and Live Life as an Optimist*. New York: Harvest Books, 2000.

Williams, Redford and Virginia Williams. *Anger Kills: 17 Strategies for Controlling the Hostility that Can Harm Your Health*. New York: Times Books, 1993.

Young, JE and JS Klosk. *Reinventing your Life*. New York: Dutton, 1993.

Step 4: Finding a Cure for the Disease to Please

Bloomfield, Harold. *The Achilles Syndrome: Transforming Your Weaknesses into Strengths*. New York: Random House, 1985.

Braiker, Harriet. *The Disease to Please: Curing the People-pleasing Syndrome*. New York: McGraw-Hill, 2002.

Ellis, Albert and Arthur Lange. *How to Keep People from Pushing Your Buttons*. Secaucus, NJ: Carol Press, 1994.

Gray, John. *How to Get What You Want and Want What You Have*. New York: HarperCollins, 1999.

Jeffers, Susan. *Feel the Fear and Do It Anyway*. New York: Ballantine Books, 1987.

LaHayne, Tim. *Why You Act the Way You Do*. Wheaton, IL: Tyndale House Publishers, 1984.

Leman, Kevin. *The Pleasers. Women Who Can't Say No—and the Men Who Control Them*. Old Tappan, NJ: Fleming H. Revell Company, 1987.

Stoddard, Alexandra. *Making Choices. Discovering the Joy in Living the Life You Want to Lead*. New York: Avon Books, 1994.

Step 5: Letting Go and Learning to Forgive

Borysenko, Joan. *Guilt is the Teacher, Love is the Lesson*. New York: Warner Books, 1990.

Britten, Rhonda. *Fearless Living: Live without Excuses and Love without Regret*. New York: Dutton, 2000.

Casarjian, Robin. *Forgiveness: A Bold Choice for a Peaceful Heart*. New York: Bantam Books, 1992.

Davis, Laura. *I Thought We'd Never Speak Again: The Road from Estrangement To Reconciliation*. New York: HarperCollins, 2002.

Jenco, Lawrence M. *Bound to Forgive: The Pilgrimage to Reconciliation of a Beirut Hostage*. Notre Dame, IN: Ave Maria Press, 1995.

Kushner, Harold. *How Good Do We Have to Be?* New York: Little, Brown and Company, 1996.

Smedes, Lewis. *Shame and Grace: Healing the Shame We Don't Deserve*. San Francisco: HarperCollins, 1993.

_____ *Forgive and Forget: Healing the Hurts We Don't Deserve*. New York: Simon and Schuster, 1984.

Simmons, Philip. *Learning to Fall: The Blessings of an Imperfect Life*. New York: Bantam Books, 2002.

Sofield, Loughlan, ST, Carroll Juliano, SHCJ and Rosine Hammett, CSC. *Design for Wholeness: Dealing with Anger. Learning to Forgive. Building*

Self-Esteem. Notre Dame, IN: Ave Maria Press, 1990.

Viorst, Judith. *Imperfect Control: Our Lifelong Struggles with Power and Surrender.* New York: Simon and Schuster, 1998.

Step 6: Connecting with Others

Beck, Aaron. *Love Is Never Enough.* New York: Harper and Row, 1988.

Bryan, Mark. *Codes of Love: How to Rethink Your Family and Remake Your Life.* New York: Pocket Books, 1999.

Buscaglia, Leo. *Love.* New York: Fawcett, 1972

_____. *Loving Each Other.* Thorofare, NJ: Slack Incorporate, 1984.

Curran, Dolores. *Traits of a Healthy Family.* Minneapolis, MN: Winston Press, 1983.

Cohen, Alan. *Have You Hugged A Monster Today?* Haiku, HI: Alan Cohen Publications, 1982.

Engel, Beverly. *Loving Him without Losing You.* New York: John Wiley and Sons, 2000.

Gaylin, William. *Rediscovering Love.* New York: Viking, 1986.

_____. *Caring.* New York: Viking, 1983.

Gilbert, Roberta. *Extraordinary Relationships: A New Way of Thinking about Human Interactions.* New York: John Wiley and Sons, 1992.

Glasser, William and Carleen Glasser. *Getting Together and Staying Together: Solving the Mystery of Marriage.* New York: HarperCollins, 2000.

Goldstein, Jan. *Life Can Be This Good.* Berkeley, CA: Conari Press, 2002.

Gottman John M. and Joan DeClaire. *The Relationship Cure: A 5-Step Guide for Building Better Connections with Family, Friends, and Lovers.* New York: Crown Publishers, 2001.

Goulston, Mark. *The 6 Secrets of a Lasting Relationship.* New York: The Berkeley Publishing Group, 2001.

Gray, John. *Men Are from Mars, Women Are from Venus.* New York: HarperCollins, 1992.

Hendrix, Harville. *Getting the Love You Want.* New York: Henry Holt and Company, 1988.

Kirshenbaum, Mira. *Too Good to Leave, Too Bad to Stay: A Step-by-Step Guide to Help You Decide Whether to Stay In or Get Out of Your Relationship.* New York: Plume 1996.

McGraw, Phil. *Relationship Rescue. A 7 Step Strategy for Recovering With Your Partner.* New York: Hyperion, 2000.

_____. *The Relationship Rescue Workbook.* New York: Hyperion, 2001.

McKay, Matthew, et. al. *How to Communicate: The Ultimate Guide to Improving Your Personal and Professional Relationships.* New York: Fine Communications, 1996.

Markman, Howard, Scott M. Stanley and Susan L. Blumberg. *Fighting for Your Marriage.* San Francisco: Jossey-Bass, 2001.

May, Gerald. *The Awakened Heart. Opening Yourself to the Love You Need.* San Francisco: HarperCollins, 1991.

Mayhall, Carole. *Words That Hurt, Words That Heal.* Colorado Springs, CO: Navpress, 1986.

Mother Teresa. *In My Own Words.* New York: Grammercy, 1997.

Paul, Jordan and Margaret. *Do I Have to Give Up Me to Be Loved by You?* Minneapolis, MN: Hazelden, 1983.

Pipher, Mary. *The Shelter of Each Other: Rebuilding Our Families.* New York: G.P. Putnam and Sons, 1996.

Real, Terrence. *How Can I Get Through to You?* New York: Scribner, 2002.

Richo, David. *How to Be an Adult in Relationships: The 5 Keys to Mindful Loving.* Boston: Shambhala, 2002.

Saint-Exupéry, Antoine de. *The Little Prince.* New York: Harcourt, 1943.

_____. *Wind, Sand, and Stars.* New York: Reynal and Hitchcock, 1939.

Satir, Virginia. *Peoplemaking.* Palo Alto, CA: Science and Behavior Books, Inc., 1972.

Smalley, Gary. *Secrets to Lasting Love: Uncovering the Keys to Life-Long Intimacy.* New York: Simon and Schuster, 2000.

_____. *Love is a Decision.* Waco, TX: Word, 1989.

Smalley, Gary and John Trent. *The Blessing.* Nashville, TN: Thomas Nelson Publishers, 1986.

_____. *The Gift of Honor.* Nashville, TN: Thomas Nelson Publishers, 1987.

Smedes, Lewis. *Caring and Commitment: Learning to Live the Love We Promise.* New York: Harper and Row, 1988.

Whitehead, Evelyn Eaton and James D. Whitehead. *Marrying Well: Stages on the Journey of Christian Marriage.* New York: Image Books, 1981.

Step 7: Casting Away Heartache

Asker, Stephanie. Plan B. *How to Get Unstuck from Work, Family and Relationship Problems.* New York: Perigee Books, 1999.

Gordon, Sol. *When Living Hurts.* New York: Dell Publishing, 1985.

Kushner, Harold. *When Bad Things Happen to Good People.* New York: Schocken Books, 1981.

Luciani, Joseph J. *Self-Coaching: How to Heal Anxiety and Depression.* New York: John Wiley and Sons, 2001.

Peale, Norman V. *The Power of Positive Thinking.* Greenwich, CT: Fawcett Publications, 1952.

Pearsall, Paul. *Toxic Success: How to Stop Striving and Start Thriving.* Makawao, Maui, HI: Inner Ocean Publishing, 2002.

Rupp, Joyce. *Your Sorrow is My Sorrow: Hope and Strength in Time of Suffering.* New York: Crossroad, 1999.

Samra, Cal and Rose. *Holy Humor.* New York: Guideposts, 1996.

Schuller, Robert H. *Possibility Living: Add Years to Your Life and Life to Your Years with God's Health Plan.* San Francisco: HarperCollins, 2000.

Seamands, David. *A Healing for Damaged Emotions.* Wheaton, IL: Victor Books, 1981.

Siegel, Bernie. *Peace, Love and Healing.* New York: Harper and Row, 1989.

Step 8: Overcoming Adversity

Bassett, Lucinda. *Life without Limits.* New York: HarperCollins, 2001.

_____. *From Panic to Power*. New York: HarperCollins, 1995.

Browne, Joy. *Getting Unstuck: 8 Simple Steps to Solving Any Problem.* Carlsbad, CA: Hay House, 2002.

Chodron, Pema. *When Things Fall Apart: Heart Advice for Difficult Times.* Boston: Shambhala, 2002.

Fox, Emmet. *Make Your Life Worth-While.* New York: HarperCollins, 1942.

Jeffers, Susan. *End the Struggle and Dance with Life.* New York: Saint Martin's Press, 1996.

_____. *Feel the Fear and Do It Anyway.* New York: Fawcett Columbine, 1987.

Keith, Kent M. *Anyway: The Paradoxical Commandments.* New York: G. P. Putnam and Sons, 2001.

King, Pat. *Scripture-Based Solutions to Handling Stress.* Liguori, MO: Liguori, 1990.

Piper, Watty. *The Little Engine that Could.* Retold from *The Pony Engine,* by Mabel C. Bragg. New York: The Platt and Munk Company, 1930.

Richman, Linda. *I'd Rather Laugh: How to be Happy Even When Life Has Other Plans for You.* New York: Warner Books, 2001.

Schuller, Robert A. *Dump your Hang-Ups without Dumping Them on Others.* Grand Rapids, MI: Fleming H. Revell, 1993.

Seligman, Martin. *Learned Optimism: The Skills to Conquer Life's Obstacles, Large and Small.* New York: Random House, 1991.

Siskind, Barry. *Bumblebees Can Fly.* Toronto, Ontario: Stoddart, 2001.

Smedes, Lewis. *A Pretty Good Person: What it Takes to Live with Courage, Gratitude and Courage.* San Francisco: HarperCollins, 1990.

Vanzant, Iyanla. *Yesterday, I Cried: Celebrating the Lessons of Living and Loving.* New York: Simon and Schuster, 1998.

Yapko, Michael D. *Hand-Me-Down Blues: How to Stop Depression from Spreading in Families.* New York: Golden Books, 1999.

Step 9: Talking with the Shepherd

Bloomfield, Harold and Robert K. Cooper. *Think Safe, Be Safe: The Only Guide to Inner Peace and Outer Security.* New York: Three Rivers Press, 1997.

Bloomfield, Harold H. and Robert B. Kory. *Inner Joy: New Strategies for Adding Pleasure to Your Life.* New York: A Jove Book, 1980.

Carlson, Richard and Benjamin Shield, eds. *Handbook for the Heart.* Boston: Little, Brown and Company, 1996.

_____. *Handbook for the Soul.* Boston: Little, Brown and Company, 1995.

Ederer, Dorothy. *A Golfer's Day with the Master: Spiritual Wisdom from the Fairway.* New York: Doubleday, 2000.

_____. *Colors of the Spirit.* New York: Doubleday, 1998.

Girzone, Joseph. *The Parables of Joshua.* New York: Doubleday, 2001.

_____. *Never Alone: A Personal Way to God.* New York: Doubleday, 1994.

Gomes, Peter J. *The Good Life: Truths that Last in Times of Need.* San Francisco: HarperCollins, 2002.

Grabner, Kenneth E. *Awake to Life: Aware of God.* Notre Dame, IN: Ave Maria Press, 1994.

Green, Thomas. *When the Well Runs Dry: Prayer Beyond the Beginnings.* Notre Dame, IN: Ave Maria Press, 1998.

Hanh, Thich Nhat. *Present Moment, Wonderful Moment: Mindfulness Verses for Daily Living.* Berkeley, CA: Parallax Press, 1990.

_____. *The Miracle of Mindfulness.* Boston: Beacon Press, 1975.

Keating, Thomas. *Intimacy with God.* New York: Crossroad, 1994.

King, Ursula. *Christian Mystics: Their Lives and Legacies throughout the Ages.* Palto Alto, CA: Hidden Springs, 2001.

Kirvin, John. *God Hunger: Discovering the Mystic in All of Us.* Notre Dame, IN: Sorin Books, 1999.

May, Gerald. *Simply Sane. The Spirituality of Mental Health.* New York: Crossroad, 1993.

Mother Teresa. *In My Own Words*. Liguori, MO: Liguori, 1996.

Peck, M. Scott. *The Road Less Traveled*. New York: Simon and Schuster, 1978.

Schuller, Robert H. *Believe in the God Who Believes in You*. Nashville, TN: Thomas Nelson Publishers, 1989.

Wicks, Robert. *Everyday Simplicity: A Practical Guide to Spiritual Growth*. Notre Dame, IN: Sorin Books, 2000.

_____. *Living a Gentle, Passionate Life*. Mahwah, NJ: Paulist Press, 1998.

_____. *Seeds of Sensitivity. Deepening Your Spiritual Life*. Notre Dame, IN: Ave Maria Press, 1995.

Zinn-Kabat, John. *Wherever You Go There You Are: Mindfulness Meditation in Everyday Life*. New York: Hyperion, 1994.

Step 10: Believing the Best is Yet to Come

Albom, Mitch. *Tuesdays with Morrie. An old man, a young man, and life's greatest lesson*. New York: Doubleday, 1997.

Brooke, Jill. *Don't Let Death Ruin Your Life*. New York: Dutton Books, 2001.

Kübler-Ross, Elisabeth. *Death: The Final Stage of Growth*. Upper Saddle River, NJ: Prentice-Hall, 1975.

_____. *On Death and Dying*. New York: Simon and Schuster, 1969.

Kübler-Ross, Elisabeth and David Kessler. *Life Lessons*. New York: Scribner, 2000.

Morris, Virginia. *Talking About Death Won't Kill You*. New York: Workman Publishing, 2001.

Sanders, Catherine. *Grief, the Morning After: Dealing with Adult Bereavement*. New York: John Wiley and Sons, 1989.

Wilkinson, Bruce. *The Prayer of Jabez*. Sisters, OR: Multnomah, 2000.

_____. *Secrets of the Vine: Breaking Through to Abundance*. Sisters, OR: Multnomah, 2001.

Wolpe, David. *Making Loss Matter: Creating Meaning in Difficult Times*. New York: Riverhead Books, 1999.

Stories that Encourage, Inspire and Challenge

Bausch, William. *A World of Stories for Preachers and Teachers.* Mystic, CT: Twenty-Third Publications, 1998.

Canfield, Jack and Mark V. Hansen. *Chicken Soup for the Soul.* Deerfield Park, FL: Health Communications, 1993.

Cavanaugh, Brian, TOR. *The Sower's Seeds: One Hundred Inspiring Stories For Preaching, Teaching and Public Speaking.* Mahwah, NJ: Paulist Press, 1990.

_____. *More Sower's Seeds: Second Planting.* Mahwah, NJ: Paulist Press, 1992.

_____. *Fresh Packet of Sower's Seeds: Third Planting.* Mahwah, NJ: Paulist Press, 1994.

_____. *Sower's Seeds Aplenty: Fourth Planting.* Mahwah, NJ: Paulist Press, 1996.

_____. *Sower's Seeds of Virtue: Stories of Faith, Hope and Love.* Mahwah, NJ: Paulist Press, 1997.

_____. *Sower's Seeds of Encouragement: 100 Stories of Hope, Humor and Healing.* Mahwah, NJ: Paulist Press, 1998.

Costello, Andrew, J. *Down to Earth But Looking Up: Stories to Lift the Spirit.* Allen, TX: Thomas More, 1999.

Dayton, Tim. *The Quiet Voice of Soul: How to Find Meaning in Ordinary Life.* Deerfield Park, FL: Health Communications, Inc.,1995.

Halberstam, Yitta and Judith Leventhal. *Small Miracles I.* Avon, MA: Adams Media Corporation, 1997.

_____. *Small Miracles II.* Avon, MA: Adams Media Corporation, 1998.

Juniper, Daniel. *Along the Water's Edge: Stories that Challenge and How to Tell Them.* Mahwah, NJ: Paulist Press, 1982.

Wharton, Paul J. *Stories and Parables for Preachers and Teachers.* Mahwah, NJ: Paulist Press, 1986.

Youngs, Bettie B. *A String of Pearls. Inspirational Stories Celebrating Resiliency of The Human Spirit.* Avon, MA: Adams Media Corporation, 2000.

Zukov, Gary. *Soul Stories.* New York: A Fireside Book, 2000.

Movies

Ken Gire writes: "A movie theater is an unlikely place to hear God. Some may say the unlikeliest of places" (*Reflections on the Movies*; Cook Communications, 2000). Yet he maintains we can discern God's voice in film when we sensitize our "eyes to see and our ears to hear" God speaking. I agree.

It's been my experience that movies are stories of our culture that provide a medium for embracing change, to removing clutter from our soul, taking control of our lives and learning to forgive, to overcoming adversity, casting away heartache and connecting with others in our journey of growth and enrichment. Here are a few with those themes:

The Rookie (2002)

Men of Honor (2000)

The Sixth Sense (1999)

The Straight Story (1999)

Les Miserables (1998)

He Got Game (1998)

Saving Private Ryan (1998)

Patch Adams (1998)

Simon Birch (1998)

The Hunchback of Notre Dame (1996)

Field of Dreams (1989)

The Dead Poets Society (1989)

The Breakfast Club (1985)

Places in the Heart (1984)

Shoot the Moon (1982)

The Elephant Man (1980)

Camelot (1969)

The Wizard of Oz (1939)

Of Related Interest...

Does Life Make Sense?
A Pastor's Ten Best Guesses About God, Life, and Love.
Joseph Breighner

These warm, witty, yet thought-provoking reflections come from a pastor who is trying to help people feel better about God, themselves, and other people.

1-58595-192-7, 96 pp, $10.95 (X-34)

I'm Still Dancing
Praying through Good Days and Bad
Rose Tillemans

These passionate, whimsical, and upbeat prayers express faith in the God of quiet gifts and of refreshment, of laughter and of justice, of refuge and of joy.

1-58595-237-0, 80pp, $9.95 (X-82)

How to Discover Your Personal Mission
The Search for Meaning
John Monbourquette

In this user-friendly book the author leads readers through a three-stage process of learning to let go of the past, deepening a sense of indentity and mission, and risking a new beginning in life.

1-58595-166-8, 200 pp, $12.95 (X-08)

How to Love Again
Moving from Grief to Growth
John Monbourquette

The author here combines psychology and spirituality in a unique manner to offer comfort in times of despair, and describes the healing process that comes after loss.

1-58595-165-X, 176 pp, $12.95 (X-07)

TWENTY-THIRD PUBLICATIONS

185 WILLOW STREET • PO BOX 180 • MYSTIC, CT 06355
TEL: 1-800-321-0411 • FAX: 1-800-572-0788
Bayard   E-MAIL: ttpubs@aol.com • www.twentythirdpublications.com